COMPUTER NETWORKS
(THEORY & PRACTICALS)

AUTHORS

Dr. Brijendra Pratap Singh
Assistant Professor,
School of Computer Science Engineering Technology, Bennett University, Greater Noida, India

Dr. Manoj Madhava Gore
Professor,
Department of Computer Science and Engineering, Motilal Nehru National Institute of Technology Allahabad, Prayagraj, India

REVIEWER

Dr. Sandeep Kumar
Associate Professor,
Computer Science and Engineering,
IIT Roorkee, Roorkee-247667,
Uttarakhand, India

KHANNA BOOK PUBLISHING CO. (P) Ltd.
4C/4344, Ansari Road, Darya Ganj,
New Delhi, India

All India Council for Technical Education
Nelson Mandela Marg, Vasant Kunj,
New Delhi, India

Dear Readers,

To prevent the piracy, this book is secured with HIGH SECURITY HOLOGRAM on the front title cover. In case you don't find the hologram on the front cover title, please write us to at contact@khannabooks.com or whatsapp us at +91-99109 09320 and avail special gift voucher for yourself.

Specimen of Hologram on front Cover title:

Moreover, there is a SPECIAL DISCOUNT COUPON for you with EVERY HOLOGRAM.

How to avail this SPECIAL DISCOUNT:

Step 1: Scratch the hologram

Step 2: Under the scratch area, your "coupon code" is available

Step 3: Logon to www.khannabooks.com

Step 4: Use your "coupon code" in the shopping cart and get your copy at a special discount

Step 5: Enjoy your reading!

ISBN: 978-93-5538-298-6

Book Code: DIP470EN

Computer Networks: Theory & Practicals

by Dr. Brijendra Pratap Singh and Dr. Manoj Madhava Gore

First Edition: 2026

Originally Published by:

All India Council for Technical Education, Ministry of Education, GOI

Exclusively Published & Distributed by:

Khanna Book Publishing Co. (P) Ltd.
4C/4344, Ansari Road, Daryaganj,
New Delhi (INDIA)

Visit us at: **www.khannabooks.com**
Write us at: **contact@khannabooks.com**

To view complete list of books, Please scan the QR Code: KPH

Printed in Bharat.

प्रो. टी. जी. सीताराम
अध्यक्ष
Prof. T. G. Sitharam
Chairman

सत्यमेव जयते

आज़ादी का अमृत महोत्सव

अखिल भारतीय तकनीकी शिक्षा परिषद्
(भारत सरकार का एक सांविधिक निकाय)
(शिक्षा मंत्रालय, भारत सरकार)
नेल्सन मंडेला मार्ग, वसंत कुंज, नई दिल्ली–110070
दूरभाष : 011–26131498
ई–मेल : chairman@aicte-india.org

ALL INDIA COUNCIL FOR TECHNICAL EDUCATION
(A STATUTORY BODY OF THE GOVT. OF INDIA)
(Ministry of Education, Govt. of India)
Nelson Mandela Marg, Vasant Kunj, New Delhi-110070
Phone : 011-26131498
E-mail : chairman@aicte-india.org

FOREWORD

Engineers are the backbone of any modern society. They are the ones responsible for the marvels as well as the improved quality of life across the world. Engineers have driven humanity towards greater heights in a more evolved and unprecedented manner.

The All India Council for Technical Education (AICTE), have spared no efforts towards the strengthening of the technical education in the country. AICTE is always committed towards promoting quality Technical Education to make India a modern developed nation emphasizing on the overall welfare of mankind.

An array of initiatives has been taken by AICTE in last decade which have been accelerated now by the National Education Policy (NEP) 2020. The implementation of NEP under the visionary leadership of Hon'ble Prime Minister of India envisages the provision for education in regional languages to all, thereby ensuring that every graduate becomes competent enough and is in a position to contribute towards the national growth and development through innovation & entrepreneurship.

One of the spheres where AICTE had been relentlessly working since past couple of years is providing high quality original technical contents at Under Graduate & Diploma level prepared and translated by eminent educators in various Indian languages to its aspirants. For students pursuing 2nd year of their Engineering education, AICTE has identified 87 books, which shall be translated into 12 Indian languages - Hindi, Tamil, Gujarati, Odia, Bengali, Kannada, Urdu, Punjabi, Telugu, Marathi, Assamese & Malayalam. In addition to the English medium, books in different Indian Languages are going to support the students to understand the concepts in their respective mother tongue.

On behalf of AICTE, I express sincere gratitude to all distinguished authors, reviewers and translators from the renowned institutions of high repute for their admirable contribution in a record span of time.

AICTE is confident that these outcomes based original contents shall help aspirants to master the subject with comprehension and greater ease.

(Prof. T. G. Sitharam)

ACKNOWLEDGEMENT

The authors are grateful to the authorities of AICTE, particularly Prof. T G Sitharam, Chairman; Dr. Abhay Jere, Vice-Chairman; Prof. Rajive Kumar, Member-Secretary, Dr. Ramesh Unnikrishnan, Advisor-II and Dr. Sunil Luthra, Director, Training and Learning Bureau for their planning to publish the books on Computer Networks: Theory & Practicals. We sincerely acknowledge the valuable contributions of the reviewer of the book Dr. Sandeep Kumar, Associate Professor, IIT Roorkee. We would like to thank Dr. Abhinav Kumar, Assistant Professor, IIIT Surat, for his valuable suggestions. We are thankful to Prof. Debahuti Mishra (Head, CSED) and Dr. Shashank Chaudhary, Dr. Dibya Rajan, Mr. Rashmi Ranjan Mohakud, and Prof. (Dr.) Manojranjan Nayak (Founder and President) Siksha 'O' Anusandhan Deemed to be University, Bhubaneswar, Odisha. We owe a lot to our discussions on the broad area of Computer Networks with Prof. Rajeev Tripathi, Prof. Neeraj Tyagi, Dr. Mayank Pandey and Dr. Shashank Shrivatav of MNNIT Allahabad, Prayagraj, India.

This book is an outcome of various suggestions of AICTE members, experts and authors who shared their opinion and thought to further develop the engineering education in our country. Acknowledgements are due to the contributors and different workers in this field whose published books, review articles, papers, photographs, footnotes, references and other valuable information enriched us at the time of writing the book.

Dr. Brijendra Pratap Singh

Dr. Manoj Madhava Gore

PREFACE

This book on "Computer Networks: Theory & Practicals" is written as a textbook for the diploma course. However, this book can be used by any interested beginner. The use of network applications and the Internet is increasing every day. It is desirable that each user should have elementary knowledge about the working of network applications and the Internet. Moreover, the professionals are supposed to know a very brief understanding of network application development, network architecture, network protocols, and network management. This book is written in such a way that a student can understand the basic concepts of networking and gets a glimpse of advanced developments related to the Internet.

This book is divided into five units. Each unit is enriched with a "know more" section and laboratory task. Each unit is interrelated to the other. This book covers computer networks, standards and administration of the Internet, network architecture and protocols, along with practicals.

Reading of Unit 1 is essential to understand the rest of the contents of this book. Unit 1 contains the computer network's historical development, standards, administration, network architecture, and communication perspective. Unit 2 explains the transmission media (wired and wireless), network topologies, data link layer, Ethernet, wireless LAN, and Bluetooth.

Unit 3 discusses the functioning of the network layer. This unit explains how a datagram from one host to another host is transmitted through the routers. The routing algorithm and routing protocols are discussed. This discussion helps students to understand the formation of a forwarding table at a router and the transmission of a datagram from one router to another router. This unit also discusses the addressing scheme (specifically Internet Protocol version 4) for end systems and routers.

Unit 4 explains the transport layer and application layer protocols and services. The transport layer provides process-to-process communication, reliable delivery, congestion control, and error control. The transmission control protocol (TCP) segment format is discussed. A network application program executes at the application layer. The application layer facilitates protocols, such as SMTP, DNS, HTTP, and FTP, for network application development. Unit 5 discusses the network devices, such as a hub, switch, router, network interface card, and Wi-Fi devices. The network management and simple network management protocol are discussed.

This book contains the practicals (laboratory task), such as network cable connection (making patch card), cable testing, the configuration of desktop & laptop (i.e., IP address, subnet mask, default gateway), working with the network interface card, hub, switch, router, and wireless access point, network simulation tool (i.e., Cisco packet tracer), simulation of a wired and wireless local area network. The book aims to make a student understand the basic concepts and make the student curious about the subject for further study.

Dr. Brijendra Pratap Singh

Dr. Manoj Madhava Gore

OUTCOME BASED EDUCATION

For the implementation of an outcome based education the first requirement is to develop an outcome based curriculum and incorporate an outcome based assessment in the education system. By going through outcome based assessments, evaluators will be able to evaluate whether the students have achieved the outlined standard, specific and measurable outcomes. With the proper incorporation of outcome based education there will be a definite commitment to achieve a minimum standard for all learners without giving up at any level. At the end of the programme running with the aid of outcome based education, a student will be able to arrive at the following outcomes:

Programme Outcomes (POs) are statements that describe what students are expected to know and be able to do upon graduating from the program. These relate to the skills, knowledge, analytical ability attitude and behaviour that students acquire through the program. The POs essentially indicate what the students can do from subject-wise knowledge acquired by them during the program. As such, POs define the professional profile of an engineering diploma graduate.

National Board of Accreditation (NBA) has defined the following seven POs for an Engineering diploma graduate:

PO1. Basic and Discipline specific knowledge: Apply knowledge of basic mathematics, science and engineering fundamentals and engineering specialization to solve the engineering problems.

PO2. Problem analysis: Identify and analyses well-defined engineering problems using codified standard methods.

PO3. Design/ development of solutions: Design solutions for well-defined technical problems and assist with the design of systems components or processes to meet specified needs.

PO4. Engineering Tools, Experimentation and Testing: Apply modern engineering tools and appropriate technique to conduct standard tests and measurements.

PO5. Engineering practices for society, sustainability and environment: Apply appropriate technology in context of society, sustainability, environment and ethical practices.

PO6. Project Management: Use engineering management principles individually, as a team member or a leader to manage projects and effectively communicate about well-defined engineering activities.

PO7. Life-long learning: Ability to analyse individual needs and engage in updating in the context of technological changes.

COURSE OUTCOMES (CO)

By the end of the course the students are expected to learn:

CO-1: Understanding of computer networks, issues, limitations, options available.

CO-2: Understanding of the care that needs to be taken while developing applications designed to work over computer networks.

CO-3: Able to configure basic LAN and connect computers to it.

CO-4: Understanding of the working of Data Link Layer, Network Layer, and Transport Layer.

CO-5: Understanding of the working of Application Layer Protocols, Domain Name System, and Network Management System.

Mapping of Course Outcomes with Programme Outcomes to be done according to the matrix given below:

Course Outcomes	EXPECTED MAPPING WITH PROGRAMME OUTCOMES (1- Weak Correlation; 2- Medium correlation; 3- Strong Correlation)						
	PO-1	PO-2	PO-3	PO-4	PO-5	PO-6	PO-7
CO-1	3	3	3	3	1	1	3
CO-2	3	2	2	2	1	1	3
CO-3	3	2	2	2	1	1	3
CO-4	3	2	2	3	1	1	3
CO-5	3	3	3	3	1	1	3

GUIDELINES FOR TEACHERS

To implement Outcome Based Education (OBE) knowledge level and skill set of the students should be enhanced. Teachers should take a major responsibility for the proper implementation of OBE. Some of the responsibilities (not limited to) for the teachers in OBE system may be as follows:

- Within reasonable constraint, they should manoeuvre time to the best advantage of all students.
- They should assess the students only upon certain defined criterion without considering any other potential ineligibility to discriminate them.
- They should try to grow the learning abilities of the students to a certain level before they leave the institute.
- They should try to ensure that all the students are equipped with the quality knowledge as well as competence after they finish their education.
- They should always encourage the students to develop their ultimate performance capabilities.
- They should facilitate and encourage group work and team work to consolidate newer approach.
- They should follow Blooms taxonomy in every part of the assessment.

Bloom's Taxonomy

Level	Teacher should Check	Student should be able to	Possible Mode of Assessment
Creating	Students ability to create	Design or Create	Mini project
Evaluating	Students ability to Justify	Argue or Defend	Assignment
Analysing	Students ability to distinguish	Differentiate or Distinguish	Project/Lab Methodology
Applying	Students ability to use information	Operate or Demonstrate	Technical Presentation/ Demonstration
Understanding	Students ability to explain the ideas	Explain or Classify	Presentation/Seminar
Remembering	Students ability to recall (or remember)	Define or Recall	Quiz

GUIDELINES FOR STUDENTS

Students should take equal responsibility for implementing the OBE. Some of the responsibilities (not limited to) for the students in OBE system are as follows:

- Students should be well aware of each UO before the start of a unit in each and every course.
- Students should be well aware of each CO before the start of the course.
- Students should be well aware of each PO before the start of the programme.
- Students should think critically and reasonably with proper reflection and action.
- Learning of the students should be connected and integrated with practical and real life consequences.
- Students should be well aware of their competency at every level of OBE.

ABBREVIATIONS AND SYMBOLS

List of Abbreviations

General Terms			
Abbreviations	**Full form**	**Abbreviations**	**Full form**
ARP	Address Resolution Protocol	ARPANET	Advanced Research Project Agency Network
AS	Autonomous System	BGP	Border Gateway Protocol
BIS	Bureau of Indian Standards	CIDR	Classless Inter-Domain Routing
DHCP	Dynamic Host Configuration Protocol	DNS	Domain Name System
FTP	File Transfer Protocol	HTTP	HyperText Transfer Protocol
IANA	Internet Assigned Numbers Authority	IAB	Internet Architecture Board
IEC	International Electrotechnical Commission	IEEE	Institute of Electrical and Electronics Engineers
IRTF	Internet Research Task Force	IP	Internet Protocol
IETF	Internet Engineering Task Force	ISO	International Organization for Standardization
ISP	Internet Service Provider	ITU	International Telecommunication Union
LAN	Local Area Network		
MTU	Maximum Transfer Unit	MSS	Maximum Segment Size
OSPF	Open Shortest Path First	OSI	Open System Interconnection
RFC	Request For Comments	PDU	Protocol Data Unit
SMTP	Simple Mail Transfer Protocol	RIP	Routing Information Protocol
SQL	Structured Query Language	SNMP	Simple Network Management Protocol
STP	Shielded Twisted Pair	SSID	Service Set Identifier
UDP	User Datagram Protocol	TCP	Transmission Control Protocol
WWW	World Wide Web	UTP	Unshielded Twisted Pair
		W3C	World Wide Web Consortium

LIST OF FIGURES

LIST OF TABLES

CONTENTS

1 Principles of Computer Networks

UNIT SPECIFICS

Through this unit we discuss the following aspects:

- History of Computer Networks Development;
- Standards and Administration for Internet;
- Computer Networks and Internet;
- Hardware and Software Perspective of Internet;
- Communication Infrastructure Perspective of Internet;
- Network Protocol Architecture;
- ISO Reference Model and TCP/IP Model.

The historical development of computer networks, standardization and administration, protocols, and network architecture are discussed for understanding, curiosity, and creativity. Multiple-choice, short, and long answer types of questions are provided for practice. References are given, which will help the learner for further readings. A learner can study them for adequate practice of the concepts. An introductory lab assignment is provided to make the student of the subject familiar with the devices. Based on the chapter context, there is a "Know More" section. The supplementary information provided in "Know More" is carefully designed so that it is beneficial for the users of the book.

RATIONALE

Student will get introductory idea of computer networks: about the development, standards, administration, protocol, and network architecture. It explains standardization organizations such as ISO, ITU, IETF, IANA, etc. The network architectures, specifically, TCP/IP Model and OSI Reference Model are discussed and compared to get a clear understanding. All these basic aspects are relevant to start learning about computer networks and the Internet properly.

PRE-REQUISITES

This unit requires no pre-requisite.

UNIT OUTCOMES

The five outcomes of this unit are given below:

U1-O1: Review of the Development of Computer Networks

U1-O2: Describe the Standards and Administration of the Internet

U1-O3: Explain Computer Network and Internet

U1-O4: Understand the Network Protocol Architecture

U1-O5: Describe OSI Reference Model and TCP/IP Model

Unit-1 Outcomes	EXPECTED MAPPING WITH COURSE OUTCOMES (1- Weak Correlation; 2- Medium correlation; 3- Strong Correlation)				
	CO-1	CO-2	CO-3	CO-4	CO-5
U1-O1	3	2	1	1	1
U1-O2	3	3	2	2	2
U1-O3	3	3	3	3	3
U1-O4	3	3	3	3	3
U1-O5	3	3	2	2	2

1.1 HISTORY OF COMPUTER NETWORKS DEVELOPMENT

Telecommunication history begins with the use of ***drums and smoke signals*** in human society. In the late 18th century, that is, the 1790s, ***semaphore systems*** emerged. It requires skilled operators and expensive towers, often at the interval of 10 to 30 km; therefore, it is very costly. A line of stations that is Towers to convey textual information ***by means of visual signals***. Claude Chappe invented a semaphore system ***in 1792 in France, which was the first semaphore system of the industrial age.***

The invention of an ***Electric Telegraph*** replaced the semaphore system. The development of communication devices with electricity started in about 1726. A successful electric telegraph was built by Francis Ronalds (English scientist and inventor) in 1816. Telegraph lines spanned over 32000 km in the United States by 1851. Most important contributions at that time were highly efficient ***Morse code***, which was co-developed with the Vail. Samuel Morse invented a method for encoding text characters as a sequence of two different signal duration, which is used in telecommunication. In 1851, a ***submarine cable*** was installed across the English Channel. In 1857, a ***transatlantic cable*** was installed.

The invention of an ***electric telephone*** happened in the 1870s. Alexander Graham Bell was an innovator. In 1886 ***wireless telephone call*** was conducted. ***Radio wave-based communication*** was established in 1901. Guglielmo Marconi and Karl Braun received a ***noble prize in physics for their contribution to wireless communication*** in 1909. Jagdish Chandra Bose (1894 -1896) investigated millimeter wave communication. He introduced the ***semiconductor to detect radio waves.***

In the 1930s, research for ***electronic television*** was started. ***Cathode Ray tube television*** is developed in the 1930s. From 1950 onwards wide use of ***semiconductor devices*** led to modern telecommunication. The concept of ***videotelephony was dreamed*** in the 1870s. Intensive research & experiments have been done in the field of electric telegraphy, telephony, radio, and television. ***Satellite for telecommunication*** was introduced in the 1960s. Advancement in the submarine cable reduces the use of satellite communication but still provides service to remote places and islands where no submarine cable.

In the 1950s, the dominant player in the communication area was ***telephone network***. The development of today's internet technologies was started by the ***project ARPANET***. This project was carried out by the Advanced Research Project Agency. ***Packet switching technology*** is invented in this period. In the 1960s, computers were very costly. Large companies, universities, and the government only have computers because of the high cost. A time-sharing system project had the goal of allowing people to harness the power of a computer. The project chooses to implement the idea of packet switching. In 1969 initially, two nodes (University of California Los Angeles (UCLA) and Stanford Research Institute (SRI)) were connected, and then two other Nodes (School of computing of the University of Utah and University of California Santa Barbara).

ARPANET was an ***overlay built on the top of a telephone network***. Other members, such as universities and government participated in ARPANET to promote research in packet switching technology, which made a large network. After ARPANET, many packet switch networks came into existence. In 1972, ***CYCLADES Network in France***. The ***idea of sliding window protocol*** came into existence from here. In 1973, ***Ethernet*** was invented at XeroxPARC. Different kinds of packet switched networks came into existence, for example, Aloha network, Ethernet, and token ring. The ***problem was how to connect different kinds of networks together***.

TCP/IP was invented to enable communication among different networks. ***Gateways*** connect the networks and translate between different network protocols. There is ***no global control management***. All these gateways will agree on one protocol and be standardized. This protocol is ***Internet Protocol*** (IP). In 1978, ***IP split into two, namely (i) IP and (ii) TCP.*** IP in the network and TCP at the end-point. Addresses of nodes are organized hierarchically. Class addresses in 80's class A, B, and C (not used anymore). In 1982, TCP/IP was standardized. Berkeley's Computer system research group developed a socket layer.

In 1983, the Athena project at MIT built a campus area network. A lot of work was done here on ***file systems, distributed file systems, Kerberos authentication schemes***, and ran TCP/IP stack. In 1984, ***Domain Name System*** was introduced. Originally, it was maintained in a file called host.txt. In the 1980s, to standardize protocol, the ***Internet Engineering Task Force*** (IETF) came into existence. In the late 1980s, Jacobson designed a ***congestion control algorithm***.

In 1991, another breakthrough came into existence, that is ***World Wide Web***. It is developed by Tim Berners Lee. In the mid-1990s, ***commercial Internet Service Providers*** (ISPs) emerged into the system. For scaling, ***classless addressing*** is adopted (longest prefix match). The introduction of network address translation came into existence. Border Gateway Protocol (BGP) was introduced among the competing internet service providers. In 1993, ***search engine development*** started. In 1998, ***content distribution network*** development started. After this, ***peer-to-peer network*** on Internet development (Gnutella, Freenet, distributed hash table Chord, BitTorrent) is started. After 2000, security threats arise. A ***Denial-of-Service attack*** happened. SQL worm attack happened. Phishing and route hijacking started.

1.2 STANDARDS AND ADMINISTRATION

Standard is required to ***establish coordination among multiple*** ideas (that is, how things should be done), device manufacturers, and service providers to avoid chaos. Standards deals with the requirements of interoperability. Internet standards are thoroughly tested specifications. A specification gets a standard status after passing through a strict procedure. A specification starts as a draft. Its lifetime is six months, and it has no official status. Upon the recommendation of the committee, a draft is published as a Request For Comments (RFC). An RFC document can be in one of the 6 maturity levels, namely (i) proposed standards, (ii) draft standards, (iii) internet standards, (iv) experimental, (v) informational, and (vi) historic. An RFC is classified into 5 requirement levels, namely, (i) not recommended, (ii) recommended, (iii) limited use, (iv) elective, and (v) required.

International standardization authorities are ***established by either treaty among governments or by a voluntary organization***. In the world of communication networks, the notable organizations are (i) International Telecommunication Union (ITU), (ii) International Organization for Standardization (ISO), (iii) Internet Engineering Task Force (IETF), (iv) Institute of Electrical and Electronics Engineers (IEEE), (v) Internet Society, (vi) Internet Architecture Board (IAB), and (vii) Internet Assigned Numbers Authority (IANA).

International Telecommunication Union (ITU): ITU was founded in 1865. Its objective is to promote and facilitate international connectivity. The United Nations does the tasks related to the Information and Communication Technology through the ITU. ITU takes care of the ***allocation of satellite orbits and the global radio spectrum***. It develops the standards for seamless interconnectivity worldwide in communication networks. Each time you access the Internet or make a phone call via mobile, you are benefiting from the work of ITU. It has mainly three sectors, namely (i) ITU-T (for standardization of the Telecommunication sector), (ii) ITU-R (for the Radio Communication sector), and (iii) ITU-D (for the development sector).

International Organisation for Standardization (ISO): This came into existence officially in 1947 with 67 technical committees (a technical committee is a group of experts). ISO is an independent ***non-governmental international organisation***. It has 167 national standards bodies as its member. Members are standards organisations in their countries. There is only ***one member per country*** in ISO.

Bureau of Indian Standards (BIS) [National Standards Body of India]: BIS is a member of ISO. ISO brings experts on one platform through its member from all over the world to develop International Standards. ISO and ITU-T are often corporate in the case of Telecommunication standards. OSI (Open System Interconnection) network model is developed by the ISO. It has many technical committees; each committee deals a particular a specific domain. ISO/IEC JTC1 works in the domain of information technology. It is created jointly with one technical committee of ISO and with one committee of IEC (International Electrotechnical Commission). IEC is also a standardization body. Each technical committee has subcommittees. A subcommittee has working groups. The work is largely done at the working group.

Institute of Electrical and Electronics Engineers (IEEE): IEEE is a technical organization. IEEE ***publishes journals and organizes conferences on technical domain***, namely electrical, electronics, and computer science. IEEE also has standardization committees. These committees ***develop standards in the field of Electrical and Computer Engineering***. For example, the IEEE 802 LAN/MAN standards committee develops networking standards. Ethernet, wireless LAN, wireless PAN, and wireless MAN standards are the most widely used.

Internet Society: The Internet Society was created in 1992 as an ***international non-profit organization***. It provides support for the process of Internet Standardization. Internet Society accomplishes this by ***cooperating among the internet administrative agencies***. These agencies are Internet Architecture Board, Internet Engineering Task Force, and Internet Research Task Force (IRTF). The internet architecture board evolved from an informal committee to oversee ARPANET development. IAB's primary purpose is to provide long-term technical direction for Internet development. The IAB is chartered as an advisory body of the internet society and a committee of the Internet Engineering Task Force (IETF).

Internet Engineering Task Force (IETF): IETF is a standards development organization for the Internet, founded in 1986. The IETF ***publishes its technical documentation as RFCs*** (Request For Comments). The work of IETF is supported by Internet Engineering Steering Group (IESG), IAB, and IRTF. IRTF addresses research issues in the domain of Internet, which are considered as long-term issues.

Internet Assigned Numbers Authority (IANA): IANA is an organisation that takes care of ***allocating unique codes*** which are used in the technical standards. IANA also manages the IP addresses allocation. IANA activities are related to domain name services, number resources (i.e., internet protocol (IP) addressing system and autonomous system numbers (used for routing internet traffic)), and protocols numbering system in cooperation with standards bodies. In the world, there are five Regional Internet Registries (RIRs). IP addresses and autonomous system numbers are managed, distributed, and registered by them.

World Wide Web Consortium (W3C): W3C is the international organization for the ***standardization of the web***. It was founded in 1994 by Tim Berners Lee. W3C develops web standards.

1.3 COMPUTER NETWORKS AND INTERNET

A computer network is an interconnection of computers for communication. Internet is a network of computer networks that interconnects billions of devices. A network is shown in Figure 1.1 in which end-systems (e.g., desktop, laptop, server), connection medium (e.g., wired, wireless), and connecting devices (e.g., switch, router) are used. To understand the Internet, there are two perspectives: (i) the components used in it, i.e., hardware and software, which constitute the Internet (ii) networking infrastructure, i.e., communication infrastructure that provides services to applications that are distributed over multiple machines.

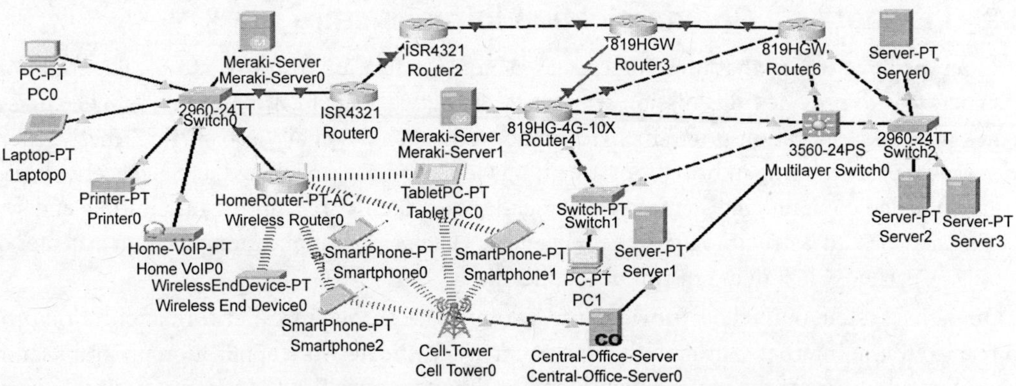

Fig. 1.1: A network of end systems using connecting devices

1.3.1 Hardware and Software Perspective

The Internet is a computer network. Billions of computing devices are interconnected in the Internet. A few decades ago, the computing machines in the network were desktop machines, Linux workstations, and server machines used for the services, such as web pages and email. However, nowadays, new devices include mobile smartphones, tablets, smart television, thermostat, security appliances, smart watches, eyeglasses, cars, traffic control systems, smart home devices, etc. In the terminology of the Internet, these computing devices are referred to as hosts or end systems. To make a connection among these end systems, we require the transmission medium and connecting device. The transmission medium may be wired (i.e., guided) or wireless (i.e., unguided). The wired transmission medium may be built using copper or optical fiber. The Wireless medium is the atmosphere and space in which electromagnetic waves can be transmitted. The data transmission rate depends on the medium type. An end system is connected to a connecting network device (e.g., packet switch, that is, network layer switch known as router and data link layer switch) with a transmission link. We can see in Figure 1.1, many end systems are interconnected with wired and wireless links through different kinds of connecting devices. The most prominent task of a packet switch is to forward a data packet from its incoming link interface to the outgoing link interface based on some criteria which lead the data packet to its destination end system.

The end system is connected to the Internet through the Internet Services Provider (ISP). The ISP which is connected to the end system is Residential Internet Service Provider, for example, telephone companies, university ISP, and Internet Service Providers that provide a connection at airports, bus stations, railway stations, hotels, shopping malls, and so on through the Wi-Fi points. ISP itself is a network of high-speed transmission links, switch, and router devices. The end system connects to an ISP with a variety of network access, namely, broadband access (for example, cable modem or Digital subscriber line), LAN access, and wireless access. The lower-tier ISP are inter-connected to the national level and international level ISP. The upper-tier ISPs are interconnected directly through high-speed fiber optic links and high-speed routers. ISP runs Internet Protocol (IP) and implements the address and naming conventions. End systems and packet switches run the protocols for the transmission of messages. TCP/IP model is known for basically for its two primary protocols (i) TCP, and (ii) IP. For interoperability, it is necessary that everyone agrees on what the protocol does. This is the point where the standards come into the scene. Organisations such as ITU, ISO, IETF, and IEEE develop the standards.

1.3.2 Internet as a Communication Infrastructure

The other perspective is that the Internet is a communication infrastructure. The task of this infrastructure is to provide transmission services to the network application programs. The end system executes network application program. The applications such as email, web surfing, messaging, real-time mapping of road traffic information, streaming videos, music, social media (e.g., Facebook, Twitter, Instagram), video conferencing, games, recommendation systems are running on multiple end systems and using network infrastructure for exchanging data. The network application program executes on the host only. A packet switch does not run the application.

Operating system of the host provides a socket interface through the network application program is connected to the Internet. Through this socket interface, the network application program sends and receives the data to/from the other network application program. For the communication among the network application program, the rules defined by the socket interface are followed. Here, the perspective is that the Internet is a communication infrastructure that provides the service of transmitting data from a network application program (executing on a source end system) to the network application program (executing on the destination end system). These hosts are connected through the socket interface.

1.4 NETWORK PROTOCOL ARCHITECTURE

A fundamental question is what stands by a protocol. In the context of a computer network, a protocol defines rules related to the structure or format of a message, specifies in which order a message can be transmitted, and specifies what actions should be taken after receiving a message. In other words, a protocol is a set of rules defining how communication is to proceed between the parties.

What is the need for protocol architecture? When devices communicate and exchange data or control among them, this task is very complex. Communication requires a very great extent of cooperation between the communicating devices. The logic for communication is not implemented as a single module. Logics are divided into subtasks and implemented into multiple small modules. These modules are arranged in a fashion called layers. Each layer performs some specific tasks which are required for the communication between the devices.

As we see the need for protocol architecture, the question arises of how looks a protocol architecture. Protocol architecture is designed as layers (a stack) of hardware and software for communication. One or more protocols are implemented at each layer of the protocol architecture. TCP/IP protocol model is one which is implemented almost everywhere in the network. Another essential protocol architecture is Open System Interconnection (OSI) model.

1.4.1 Open System Interconnection (OSI) Reference Model

The development of the OSI model protocol architecture is done by the International Organisation of Standardization (ISO). OSI reference model divides network architecture into seven layers. The criteria for making a distinct layer are based on the following: (i) a new layer is introduced when different abstraction is required (ii) a layer should be introduced in such a way that information exchange across the layer is minimised (iii) the number of layers is decided in such a way that the layer does not contain many distinct functionalities (which makes the number of layers small) and also does not contain very fewer functionalities (which makes the number of layers large) (iv) each layer performs well-defined functionalities.

1. **Physical Layer**

   Physical layer concerns to the communication channels (physical medium) to send/receive raw bits. The physical layer is concerned with the questions such as how to represent 1 and 0 using an electrical signal, how long nanoseconds a bit lasts, how to establish the initial connection, how to close the connection, what should be the number of pins in the connector, what each pin is used for, and whether the transmission is simultaneously in both directions or not.

2. **Data Link Layer**

   Data link layer concerns with the taking data from upper layer and adding header information to the packet and transmit to the physical layer at the sender host. Data link layer receives the packet from the physical layer at the receiver host. The task of the data link layer is to fragment and assemble (i.e., break and combine) the packet to meet the transmission capacity of the hardware. The receiver sends acknowledgment to the sender on the receipt of each data frame. The data link layer deals with the issue of the coordination between fast and slow sender and receiver. To deal with this, a traffic regulation mechanism is required. In the shared channel networks (e.g., broadcast networks), issues of control of the shared channel are also taken care of by this layer. A special sub-layer in the data link layer is developed to deal with this, called the medium access control sublayer.

3. **Network Layer**

   A packet is forwarded from a source end system to the destination end system. A network path is required, which is followed by the packet for the transmission. The network layer task is to determine a path in a network. Handling congestion in the network with the help of a higher layer is also the task of the network layer. The network layer also takes care of the quality-of-service of the network, such as delay, transmit time, and jitter. It also deals with the interconnection of the heterogeneous network. If you are configuring a broadcast network, finding a route is irrelevant or even non-existent.

4. **Transport Layer**

   The transport layer receives packet from the network layer and sends to the session layer. It also takes packet from session layer and transmit it to the network layer. It breaks up the data into smaller units if required. It ensures the correct order of the packets at the receiving end. Moreover, its task is to do these in such a manner that it separates the upper and lower layers, which may be changed due to hardware advancement over time.

   The type of service is also managed by the transport layer. First type of service provided by the transport layer is errorless connection between the network application program and guarantees ordered delivery i.e., the data packets are delivered to the receiver network application program in same order as it transmitted by the sender network application program. The second transport service sends isolated messages or data without a guarantee about the delivery order. Third is broadcasting messages to multiple destination hosts. It is an end-to-end layer protocol that is the source end system's network application program to the destination end system's network application program.

5. **Session Layer**

   A session is established between the communicating entities by the session layer. The session layer is responsible for controlling dialogue (that is maintaining records and managing the turn of sender and receiver for data transmission), preventing the simultaneous critical operations by two or more users using token, and synchronisation (checkpointing the long transmission helps fast recovery in case of failure).

6. **Presentation Layer**

   The data, which is going to be transmitted, has some structure, commonly known as the syntax of the data. The data also have some meaning, known as semantics. The presentation layer takes care of the structure and meaning of the data which is being communicated on a network. Computers or devices may have a different structure (representation) of data internally, but they communicate on the network with the help of the presentation layer. The data representation structure is an exchange in an abstract way. It uses encoding.

7. **Application Layer**

   The task of the application layer is to provide or define protocols that the users need to make a network application. The protocol at the application layer basically defines how an application program on the network will request and respond to data communication and define the message structure and its meaning. Application layer protocol plays a vital role in network application developments.

1.4.2 TCP/IP Model

The TCP/IP has roots in the project ARPANET. ARPANET project was a research project which was working on packet switching technology. ARPANET has grown and connected to many Universities and government systems. It used telephone lines for connection. A problem occurred after adding satellites and radio networks to it. The existing protocol was not working. Therefore, a new architecture was needed to connect different kinds of networks. The new protocols were developed, namely, TCP and IP. This new architecture is known as TCP/IP reference model. The one goal was that the connections between sender and receiver remain intact even though some of the devices or transmission links failed.

1. **Link Layer**

   In the TCP/IP protocol architecture, link layer lies at the bottom of the stack. It is a connectionless layer. The link layer describes what must be supported by your physical link to meet the requirement of a connectionless internet layer. In other words, it is an interface between a host and a transmission link. An example of link layer protocol is Ethernet.

2. **Internet Layer**

   The internet layer injects packets from the upper layer into the network and lets them travel to their destination host. Data packets traverse through multiple switches and routers; therefore, it is possible that some packets may reach later than the other which were sent after those data packets at source. By this, out of order delivery phenomena happens. The transport layer rearranges those packets if required. The internet layer describes the packet format and protocol. This is Internet Protocol (IP). Internet layer describes protocols for routing of data packets, which are maintained in routers. The objective of the internet layer is to transmit the packets to whatever destination it supposed to go.

3. **Transport Layer**

   For a conversation between two software entities (i.e., application programs) over a network, the transport layer defines and implements protocols. The transport layer defines two protocols for end-to-end connection (here, end-to-end meaning is that application programs which are running on the end system; the network layer also provides end-to-end delivery of packets but not to the application programs; many application programs run on a host). These two protocols are Transmission Control Protocol (TCP) and User Datagram Protocol (UDP). TCP is a protocol that implements reliable packet transmission that delivers a byte stream from the source machine to the destination machine anywhere on the Internet without an error. A Byte stream is segmented by the TCP, and a TCP header is added, then the segment is sent to the lower layer, i.e., the internet layer. TCP at the destination end system reassembles these segments in the correct order and sends them to the application layer as an output stream. Flow control is implemented in TCP so that it protects a slow receiver from being swamped by a fast sender. The transport layer also defines and implements a connectionless and unreliable protocol, named user datagram protocol. Applications where prompt delivery is important, like speed for video transmission, use UDP.

4. **Application Layer**

   Session layer and presentation layer are not in the TCP/IP protocol stack. The application program itself includes a session and presentation layer if required. Many of the applications have very little use for these functionalities. Protocols, which are required for network application development, for example, applications such as file transfer, domain name system, electronic mail, and world wide web use the FTP, DNS, SMTP, and HTTP protocols, respectively, are part of the application layer.

1.5 A COMPARATIVE OBSERVATION OF OSI AND TCP/IP MODEL

The first observation is that the OSI reference model and the TCP/IP model consist of seven layers and four layers, respectively, as depicted in Figure 1.2. The second observation is that the OSI reference model advocates for (i) connection-oriented packet transmission, as well as (ii) connectionless packet transmission in the network layer. In comparison, the network layer in the TCP/IP reference model implements only the connectionless transmission of a packet. The third observation is that the transport layer of the OSI model advocates for only connection-oriented communication; however, the transport layer of the TCP/IP model implements both connection-oriented and connectionless communication. The fourth observation is that TCP/IP protocol stack does not separate physical and data link layers. The physical layer is concerned with the transmission characteristics of the physical link, for example, copper wire, fiber optic medium, and wireless medium. The task implemented in the link layer is to control frames to send them from one device to another. The link layer also takes care of the desired degree of reliability of the frame transmission.

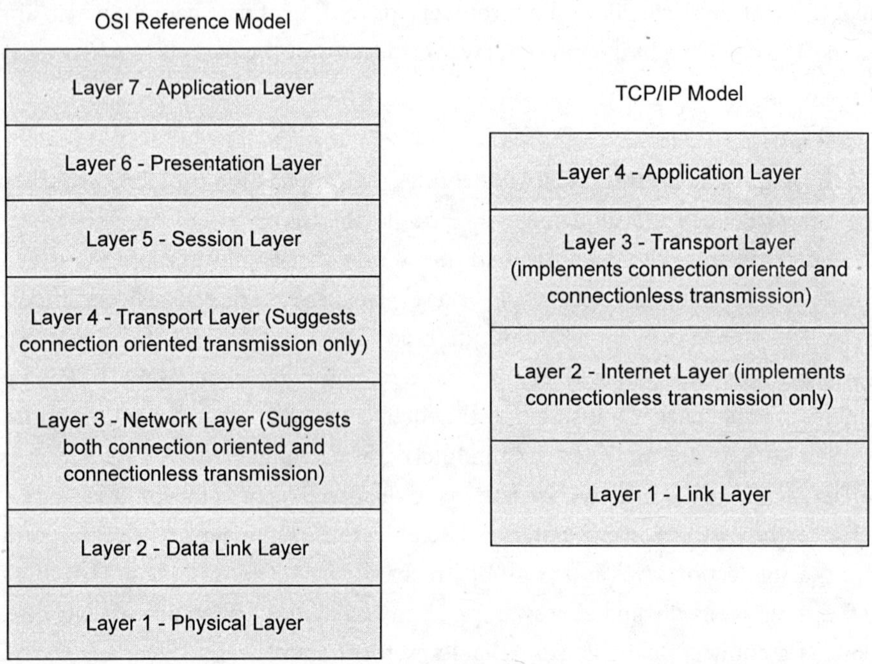

Fig. 1.2: Comparative analysis of OSI and TCP/IP model

UNIT SUMMARY

This unit describes a brief history of the development of computer networks and the Internet. The most important development was the development of Internet Protocol and Transmission Control Protocol which paved the way to connect multiple networks which are using different technologies. The idea of packet switching was introduced to share the computing power of machines among multiple users who are geographically distant. ARPANET was an overlay network created on the top of a telephone network that makes use of the packet switching concept. In the 1980s, the idea of the sliding window protocol came into existence. In the 1980s, Ethernet was invented. Different kinds of packet switch networks came into existence, for example, Aloha network, Ethernet, and token ring. These different networks are connected together with the help of Internet Protocol (IP), which was invented to enable communication among different networks. In the late 1980s, Van Jacobson designed a congestion control algorithm. In 1991, World Wide Web was developed by Tim Berners Lee. After this, many applications like web, e-commerce, and peer-to-peer communication came into existence. After 2000, security threats also arise, like denial-of-service attacks, SQL warm attacks.

The standardization and administration organizations for telecommunication and the Internet are ITU, ISO, IETF, IRTF, IEEE, IEC, Internet Society, IAB, IANA, and W3C. The elements of the computer networks are hardware and software such as desktop machines, laptops, Linux workstations, server machines for web pages and email service, mobile smartphones, tablets, thermostats, security appliances, smart home appliances, etc. These machines are referred to as a host or an end system in the Internet. These end systems are connected through transmission links and packet switches. These transmission links are of many types, such as coaxial cable, copper wire, optical fiber, and radio spectrum. End systems are connected to the Internet by having a connection to an ISP. An application program running on the end system is connected to the Internet through a socket interface. Through this socket interface, the end system program sends/receives the data to/from the Internet infrastructure for the application program executing on an end system. The two most important network architectures are OSI and TCP/IP Models. The model discusses the work and tasks performed by each layer.

EXERCISES

Multiple Choice Questions (MCQ)

1. Which of the following is not an organization for Standards and Administration?
   (a) ISO (b) TCP (c) IETF (d) IAB
2. Who invented the congestion control algorithm?
   (a) Van Jacobson (b) Tim Berners Lee
   (c) Alan Turing (d) Barbara Liskov
3. Which of the following is not an end system?
   (a) Router (b) Laptop
   (c) Mobile smartphone (d) Web Server
4. From the given options find out which is not a protocol?
   (a) HTTP (b) FTP (c) TCP (d) IAB

5. Who invented the World Wide Wab?
   (a) Leslie Lamport (b) Tim Berners Lee
   (c) Abhay Bhushan Pandey (d) Linus Torvalds
6. OSI model consists of layers ?
   (a) 9 (b) 6 (c) 7 (d) 3
7. TCP/IP reference model consists of layers?
   (a) 4 (b) 3 (c) 5 (d) 6
8. What is the full form of ISO?
   (a) International Standards Office
   (b) International Organization for Standardization
   (c) Organization for International Standards
   (d) International Standards Organization
9. Which one of the following is not an application layer protocol?
   (a) DNS (b) SMTP (c) HTTP (d) TCP
10. What is the full form of IEEE?
   (a) Institute of Electrical and Electronics Engineers
   (b) Institution for Electrical and Electronics Engg.
   (c) Information of Electrical and Ethernet Engineering
   (d) Information of Email, Ethernet, Energy

ANSWERS															
1.	(b)	2.	(a)	3.	(a)	4.	(d)	5.	(b)	6.	(c)	7.	(a)	8.	(b)
9.	(d)	10.	(a)												

Questions (Short Answer)

1. Differentiate and describe host and end system?
2. Is there any central authority that controls the Internet?
3. What is the role of IANA?
4. What is the purpose of Internet standardization?
5. What is the purpose of protocol architecture?
6. What is a protocol?
7. Describe the working of the transport layer of the OSI model.
8. Write names of five application layer protocols.
9. What is the difference between the transport layer tasks of the OSI and TCP/IP models?
10. In the TCP/IP model, where is the tasks of the session layer and presentation layer implemented?

Questions (Long Answer)

1. Describe the computer networks and Internet development history in detail.
2. Describe the following: ITU, ISO, IETF, IANA, and IEEE.
3. Write a brief note on computer networks and the Internet.
4. Compare the ISO reference model and TCP/IP model.

PRACTICAL

Aim

Showing various types of networking cables and connectors, identifying them in the Lab

Cables:

1. Ethernet Cable
2. Coaxial Cable
3. Fiber Optic Cable

Connectors:

1. Ethernet Cable Connector
2. Coaxial Cable Connector
3. USB Connector
4. Fiber Optic Cable Connector

KNOW MORE

Data Center and Cloud

A data center is a cluster of computing machines for storage and processing. Big Internet companies, such as Google, Microsoft, Amazon, and Alibaba have established data centers. A data center may consist of 10 to 100 thousand hosts. Hosts in a data center are connected through a complex computer network. The data centers are the backbone for many of the Internet applications we use frequently. For example, Amazon's e-commerce web pages are hosted at data centers. A data center provides a massively parallel computing infrastructure. A data center also provides a platform for cloud computing. Many Internet-based companies do not establish their own data center. They run their services on the cloud.

REFERENCES AND SUGGESTED READINGS

1. Andrew S. Tanenbaum, Computer Networks, 5th Edition, PHI
2. W. Richard Stevens, TCP/IP Illustrated, Volume-1, Addision Wesley, Second Edition
3. James F. Kurose and Keith W. Ross, Computer Networking: A Top–Down Approach, Pearson, Eight Edition
4. Behrouz A. Forouzan and Firouz Mosharraf, Computer Networks: A Top-Down Approach, Mc Graw Hill Education, Special Indian Edition 2012
5. William Stalling, Computer Networking with Internet Protocols and Technology, Pearson Education, First Edition

Dynamic QR Code for Further Reading

2 Transmission Media, Data Link Layer, and Local Area Networks

UNIT SPECIFICS

Through this unit we discuss the following aspects:

- Transmission Medium;
- Wired Medium;
- Wireless Medium;
- Network topologies;
- Data Link Layer;
- Ethernet;
- Wireless LAN;
- Bluetooth;
- Switching Techniques.

In this unit medium for transmitted data from one device to another device is discussed. The transmission medium is wired and wireless. The wired medium varies from copper cable to optical fiber cable. In the wireless medium, the electromagnetic spectrum is divided into many frequencies band. Different frequency bands are discussed in this unit. End system (host) and network connecting devices are connected in some fashion physically to make a network, referred as topology. This unit discusses the important topologies which are used in today's network construction. After the physical connection through the medium and connecting devices, the software that handle the communication comes into the scene. This unit discusses the data link layer which performs communication between two adjacent devices. This unit discusses the local area network technologies, namely Ethernet, Wireless LAN, and Bluetooth. This unit contains questions for practice. This also provides references for further reading. There is a "Know More" section carefully designed that gives supplementary information based on the context of this unit. A laboratory task is included to get acquainted with the wires and connecting devices to make a local area network.

RATIONALE

This unit on transmission media, topology, and local area network helps students to get a primary idea about the connections of the computers and connecting devices. The student will know how a message from the upper layer is converted to a frame, how physical addresses are used to transmit a frame by learning the data link layer. Specific local area network technologies, such as Ethernet, Wi-Fi, and Bluetooth are discussed, so that students will be able to configure and create a LAN.

PRE-REQUISITES

This unit requires the knowledge of Unit 1 of this book.

UNIT OUTCOMES

The outcomes of this unit are given below:

U2-O1: Description of Transmission Medium
U2-O2: Explanation of Wired Medium
U2-O3: Explanation of Wireless Medium
U2-O4: Description of Network Topologies
U2-O5: Description of Data Link Layer
U2-O6: Explanation of Ethernet
U2-O7: Explanation of Wireless LAN
U2-O8: Explanation of Bluetooth
U2-O9: Description of Switching Techniques

Unit-2 Outcomes	EXPECTED MAPPING WITH COURSE OUTCOMES (1- Weak Correlation; 2- Medium correlation; 3- Strong Correlation)				
	CO-1	CO-2	CO-3	CO-4	CO-5
U2-O1	2	2	3	3	3
U2-O2	2	2	2	2	2
U2-O3	2	2	3	3	3
U2-O4	2	2	3	3	3
U2-O5	2	2	2	2	2
U2-06	2	3	3	3	3
U2-07	2	3	3	3	3
U2-08	2	2	3	2	2
U2-09	1	2	2	1	1

2.1 TRANSMISSION MEDIA

A physical path is referred to a transmission medium through which the electromagnetic wave travels. The communication is done by transmitting the electromagnetic wave from sender to receiver. Transmission media are classified into two categories (i) guided media and (ii) unguided media. The characteristics of the guided media is that the waves are going along a solid medium, i.e., guided with the solid medium; These solid media are twisted pair cable, coaxial cable, and fiber optic cable. Medium such as the atmosphere and outer space, which provides the means to transmit electromagnetic wave but not guide them is referred to as unguided medium. The rate of the data transmission is decided by both the characteristics of medium as well as of the signal. The key concern related to a data transmission system is distance and data rate. The design factors of a transmission medium and signal are (i) bandwidth, (ii) transmission impairment, (iii) interference, and (iv) number of nodes (i.e., sender and receiver).

Bandwidth: The more bandwidth gives a high data rate (if all the other factors remain constant, i.e., keeping the other factor the same).

Transmission impairments: Two devices are connected with some transmission mediums. The maximum distance between the devices depends on the transmission medium. A transmission distance of a medium is highly dependent on impairments, such as attenuation. Impairments in twisted pair cables are more than coaxial cables. Impairments in coaxial cables are more than fiber optic cable.

Interference: It is a problem, mainly in unguided transmission media. However, in guided media also, interference occurs due to nearby cables. For example, twisted pair cables are often bundled together, due to which interference occurs. Shielding of a guided medium reduces the interference. Signals get distorted or wiped out if signals transmitted in the medium interfere with them. Interference is a phenomenon in which two or more waves are superimposed. The superimposed waves (the resulting wave) may have more, lower, or the same amplitude.

Number of nodes (i.e., the sender and receivers): A point-to-point connection can be made using a guided medium. A shared link can also be made using a guided medium by adding multiple senders and receivers. In the shared link, attenuation and distortion are observed, which reduces the distance and/or data rate. **Table 2.1** presents some of the commonly used frequency ranges of electromagnetic waves.

Table 2.1: Electromagnetic wave spectrum for the telecommunication

Medium	Frequency Range	Wavelength (Meters)	Wave Name
Optical fiber cable	10^{14} - 10^{15} (Hz)	10^{-5} – 10^{-6}	near infrared and visible
Coaxial cable	10^{3} – 10^{9}	10^{5} - 1	radio
Twisted pair cable	10^{2} - 10^{8}	10^{6} - 10	radio
Terrestrial and satellite transmission	10^{9} - 10^{11}	10^{-1} – 10^{-2}	microwave
FM radio and TV	10^{8} - 10^{9}	10 - 1	radio
AM radio	10^{6} - 10^{7}	10^{3} - 10^{2}	radio
Laser guided missiles	10^{12} - 10^{14}	10^{-3} – 10^{-5}	infrared

2.1.1 Wired Transmission Medium

It is also referred as guided medium. The transmission capacity of medium is observed as data rate or bandwidth. The capacity depends on the factors that the medium is connected one to one or shared into multiple systems and the distance. Twisted pair, coaxial, and fiber optic cable are widely used wired media. Twisted pair copper cable is least expensive. **Figure 2.1** shows that a twisted pair cable. A pair is used to create one link. Generally, a cable is made consisting of a number of wire pairs, wrapped by plastic cover. Hundreds of wire pair may be grouped into one cable. Each wire is twisted. Twist length of wire pairs are different. Crosstalk interferences is reduced by twisting wires.

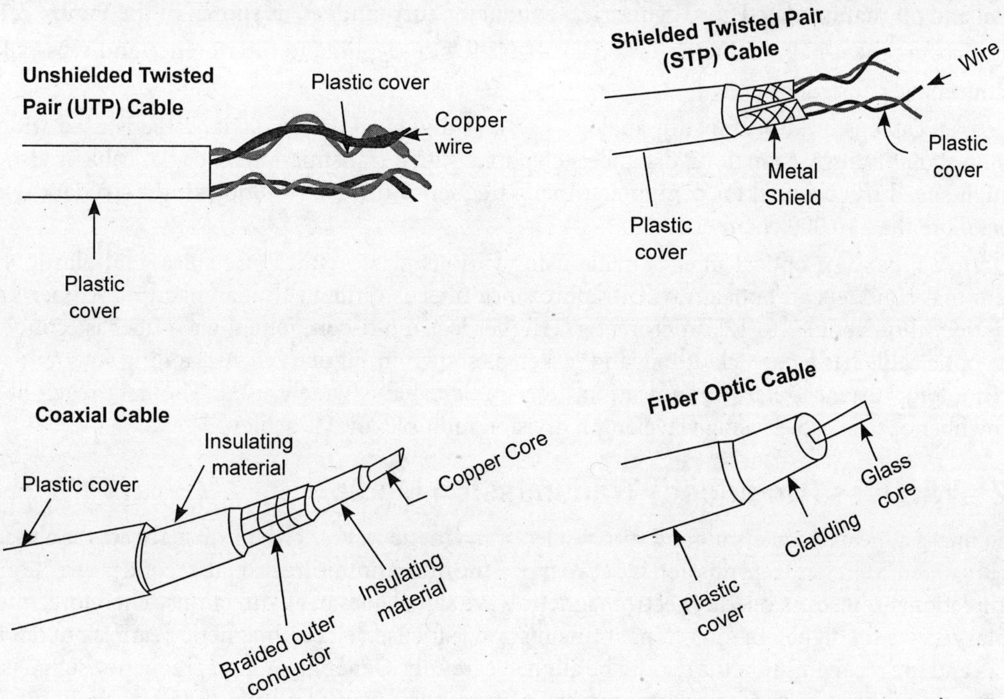

Fig. 2.1: Wired media

Twisted pair cables may be used for transmitting both digital and analog signals. It requires amplifiers and repeaters every 2 to 3 kilometers and 5 to 6 kilometers for digital and analog signal transmission, respectively. Twisted pair cable has limited bandwidth, data rate, and distance. Attenuation increases when the frequency of the wave increases very high. Twisted pair cable is susceptible to electromagnetic field, noise, and interference. Shielding the twisted pair of wires with metallic braid or sheathing reduces interference. The low-frequency interference is reduced by twisting the wire pair, and crosstalk is reduced by making twist lengths of the wire pairs different.

Unshielded Twisted Pair (UTP) Cable: It is two insulated copper wires twisted without any insulation or shielding, called a twisted pair, as shown in **Figure 2.1.** UTP cables are widely used for local area networks within a college, university, etc. Data rates in local area network using twisted wire ranges from 10 Mbps to 10 Gbps. The data rate of 10Gbps can be achieved using Category 6a cable for 100 metres. Four twisted wire pairs present in category 5 cable. 100 Mbps Ethernet local area network uses 2 out of 4 pairs, 1 Gbps Ethernet uses all 4 pairs.

Shielded Twisted Pair (STP) Cable: Twisted pair wire has extra insulation of metal foil (or it can be braided mesh). This extra insulation covers each pair of wires, as shown in the **Figure 2.1**. Shielding improves the transmission rate and prevents noise and crosstalk, but it is very expensive.

Coaxial cable: Coaxial cable is operated to transmit signals which takes a wide range of electromagnetic wave frequencies. It has two conductors. The inner core is insulated by a dielectric material and on that insulated core cylindrical conductor surrounds it, as shown in the **Figure 2.1.** An insulator covers the outer conductor. Coaxial cable is less susceptible to interference and crosstalk due to its concentric construction.

Coaxial cable is used to transmit analog as well as digital signals. Coaxial cable is used widely in television signal transmission, long distances telephone signal transmission. Coaxial cable is also used for a high-speed I/O channel for computers. Using frequency division multiplexing a coaxial cable can support more than 10,000 channels.

Optical Fiber: An optical fiber is made using various glasses, ultrapure silica, and plastic. It is a medium that conducts an optical ray. Ultrapure silica fiber is difficult to manufacture. A fiber optical cable is very thin, about 2 to 125 micrometers. Higher loss multi-component glass fiber is economical. A fiber optic cable has a core, cladding, and jacket, as shown in **Figure 2.1**. A cladding surrounds each fiber. In a long-distance telecommunication, fiber optic cable is widely used. The data reach of 1600 Gbps by fiber optical cable (using wavelength division multiplexing) is achieved.

2.1.2 Wireless (Unguided) Transmission Media

An antenna is a means to transmit and receive electromagnetic waves. The air or space acts as a medium and is unguided. Wireless transmission is of two types; the first is omnidirectional, second is directional. In omnidirectional transmission, the electromagnetic wave signal goes in all directions. Therefore, multiple antennas receive the signal. In directional transmission, a focused electromagnetic beam is put out by an antenna and the receiving antenna should be aligned carefully. Generally, a high-frequency signal is used for a directional beam. Electromagnetic waves of frequencies from 2 gigahertz (GHz) to 40 gigahertz (GHz) are referred to as microwaves. The high frequencies of electromagnetic waves are appropriate for transmission in point-to-point connection. For satellite communications, microwave is appropriate. For the omnidirectional, 30 megahertz (MHz) to one gigahertz (GHz) frequency electromagnetic waves (referred to as radio waves) are suitable.

Microwave covers some ultra high frequencies and all the super high frequencies bands. Radio wave covers the Very High Frequencies (VHF) and is part of the Ultra High Frequencies (UHF) band. Infrared wave is also used in local point-to-point and multipoint communication.

Medium Frequency (MF) Band: Electromagnetic waves of frequency range band 300 kilohertz (kHz) to 3000 kilohertz (kHz) are referred to as medium frequency bands. The transmission capacity of a medium is measured in terms of bandwidth and data rate. The transmission capacity of this band is 4 kilohertz (kHz) (bandwidth) and 10 bps (bits per second) to 1000 bps (data rate). MF band is mainly used in commercial AM (amplitude modulation) radio.

High Frequency (HF) Band: The electromagnetic wave of frequency band 3 megahertz (MHz) to 30 megahertz (MHz) is referred to as a high-frequency band. It is mainly used in short-wave radio and citizen band (CB) radio. It supports a bandwidth and data rate of 4 kilohertz (KHz) and 10 bps to 3000 bps, respectively.

Very High Frequency (VHF) Band: The electromagnetic wave of the frequency band 30 megahertz (30MHz) to 300 megahertz (300MHz) is referred to as a very high-frequency band. It is mainly used in VHF television and FM (frequency modulation) radio. It supports a bandwidth of 5 megahertz (5MHz) and a data rate of up to 100 kbps.

Ultra High Frequency (UHF) Band: The electromagnetic wave of the frequency band 300 megahertz (300 MHz) to 3000 megahertz (3000 MHz) is referred to as ultra-high frequency band. It is used in UHF television and terrestrial microwave communication. It supports a bandwidth of 20 megahertz (20 MHz) and 10 Mbps data rate.

Super High Frequency (SHF) Band: The electromagnetic wave of frequency band 3 gigahertz (3 GHz) to 30 gigahertz (30 GHz) is referred to as super high frequency band. It is primarily used in satellite telecommunication. It supports a bandwidth of 500 megahertz (500 MHz) and 100 Mbps data rate.

Extremely High Frequency (EHF) Band: The electromagnetic wave of frequency band 30 gigahertz (30 GHz) to 300 gigahertz (300 GHz) is referred to as extremely high frequency band. It is used for short point-to-point communication. It supports a bandwidth of one gigahertz (1 GHz) and 750 Mbps data rate.

K_U Band: The electromagnetic wave of frequency band 12 gigahertz (12 GHz) to 18 gigahertz (18 GHz) is referred to as K_U band. It is fully contained in the SHF band. It is primarily used in satellite communications.

Radio Wave: In informal terms, the electromagnetic wave of frequency band 3 kilohertz (3 kHz) to one gigahertz (1 GHz) is referred to as a radio wave. In general terms, it encompasses electromagnetic waves ranging from 3 kilohertz (3kHz) to 300 gigahertz (300 GHz). It contains the MF band, HF band, VHF band, and part of the UHF band.

Microwave: It is the electromagnetic wave of frequency band One gigahertz (1 GHz) to 300 gigahertz (300 GHz). It contains part of the UHF band, SHF band, and EHF band.

Infrared Wave: The electromagnetic wave of the frequency band 300 gigahertz (300 GHz) to 4 x 10^{14} Hertz (i.e., 400000 GHz; 1 GHz = 10^9 Hertz). These waves cannot penetrate walls. It is used in television (TV) remote control.

2.2 NETWORK TOPOLOGIES

The transmission media is used to connect the devices for telecommunication. The connection architectures are known as network topology. These network topologies are bus, tree, ring, and star, which are used mainly in a local area network.

Bus Topology: A bus is a multipoint medium to which multiple computer systems/hosts/endpoints are connected through a hardware interfacing tap. A bus topology is shown in **Figure 2.2.** A host sends data to the bus through the connected interfacing tap. The data transmitted by a host propagates in the bus in both directions, and all the connected hosts receive the data. A terminator is attached where bus terminates i.e., at end. The purpose of the terminator is to absorb signals and removes them from the bus.

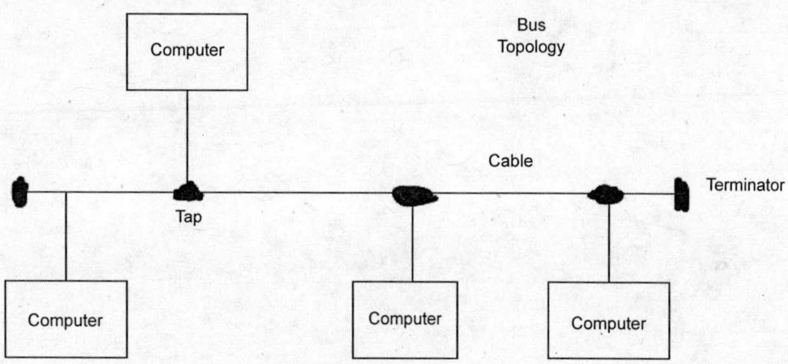

Fig. 2.2: Bus topology

Tree Topology: Tree topology contains many bus topologies. It is a generalization of bus. A tree topology is shown in **Figure 2.3**. Tree topology begins at a point called a headend. At a headend, multiple branches of cable start. A branch cable may have another branch and so on. In a tree topology also, data sent by any host propagates in the whole tree and is received by all the hosts.

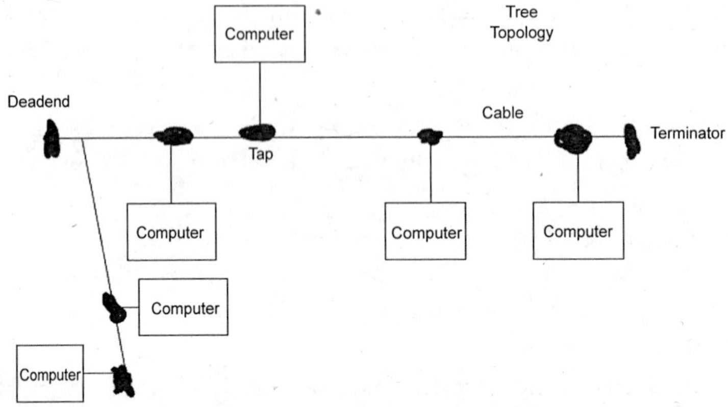

Fig. 2.3: Tree topology

Due to the shared medium in a bus and tree topology, all the hosts in the topology received each transmission data from every host. A mechanism is required to indicate for which host the data is intended. A regulation mechanism is required to manage the transmission among all hosts to avoid the collision of signals in the bus or tree (the mechanism is referred to as medium access control).

Ring Topology: A ring is formed using repeaters by connecting them point-to-point in closed form. A host or end system is connected to the repeater. The task of a repeater is to receive data from one link and transmit it to the other link bit by bit. In a ring topology, shown in **Figure 2.4**, the link is unidirectional. When a host transmits a frame (data) to another host in a ring topology, the frame moves through the repeater and link. The destination host copies frames at the repeater to which it is connected. Every repeater simply forwards the frame from its link. A frame stops moving when it comes again at the sender host's repeater. A link in the ring is shared among multiple hosts; therefore, a medium access control is required.

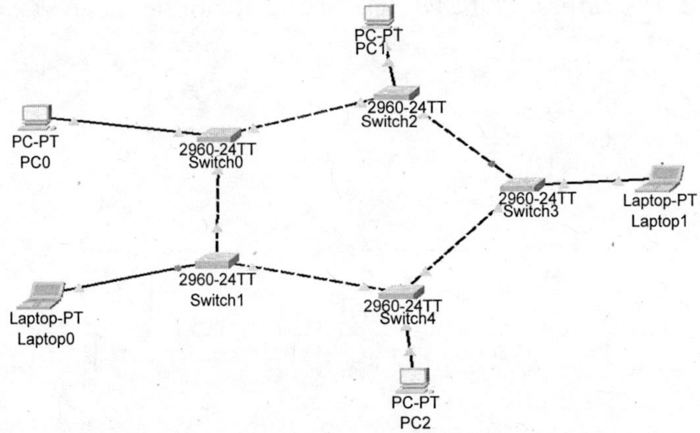

Fig. 2.4: Ring topology

Star Topology: A star topology is formed by connecting hosts to a central device (typically a switch or hub), as shown in **Figure 2.5**. There are two ways for the central device to behave; the first way is that it may simply receive a frame from a host and transmit it to all the other hosts; here, the topology logically acts as a bus even though it is physically arranged as a star. The second way is that the central device transmits a frame to the intended destination host only. In the second way, it is acting as a star topology logically too. There is a topology in which all hosts have direct connections to all other hosts, termed mesh topology. If you create your network having multiple topologies, it is termed hybrid topology.

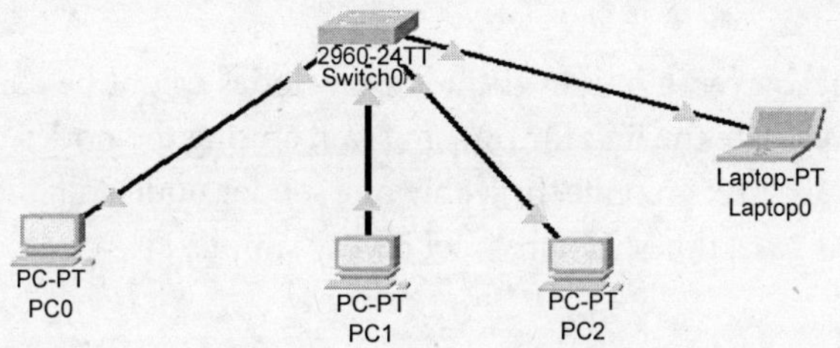

Fig. 2.5: Star topology

2.3 DATA LINK LAYER

To understand concepts here, we refer to any device as a node if it runs a data link layer protocol. Therefore, a node can be a host, switch, router, or WiFi access point. We refer to the transmission medium as a link that connects the adjacent node. Let us take an example as shown in **Figure 2.6,** laptop A transmits a message to server B. This message (datagram) will pass through the six links: (i) link 1 - WiFi link (wireless transmission medium which is shared among multiple nodes), (ii) link -2 (Ethernet link connects the WiFi access point to the switch), (iii) link - 3 (a link between switch and router), (iv) link – 4 (a link between router and router), (v) link - 5 (Ethernet link connecting router and switch), and (vi) link - 6 (Ethernet link connecting switch and server).

Here, we can observe that segment 1 as shown in the **Figure 2.6** is a wireless link managed with a different data link layer protocol than segment 2, which is managed by Ethernet protocol. It simply means that the communication from a sender host to destination host may pass through different data link layer protocols.

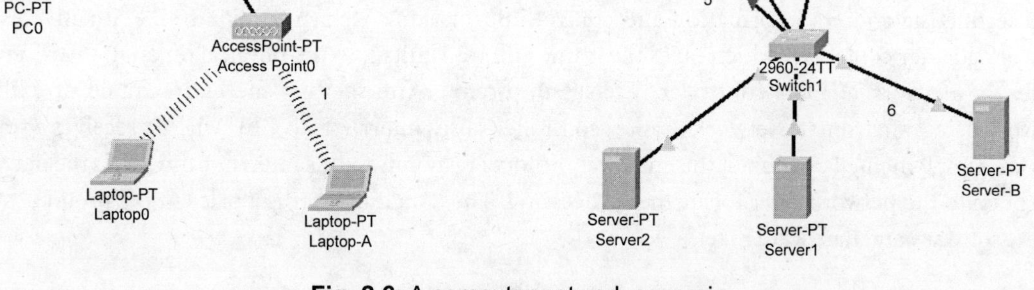

Fig. 2.6: A computer network scenario

Data link layer performs the task of transporting a network datagram (i.e., IP datagram packet) to the adjacent node, i.e., node to adjacent node transmission. The data link layer protocol provides services such as (i) framing, (ii) link access, (iii) reliable delivery, and (iv) error detection & correction.

Framing: Link layer protocol takes packets from network layer and encapsulates it into a frame. A frame is a control bit of information used by the link layer protocol along with the datagram. Different link layer protocols may have different frame formats. For example, Ethernet and 802.11 wireless LAN have different frame formats.

Link Access: At physical layer, a link to the adjacent nodes might be shared by multiple nodes. A set of rules is specified to regulate the link for transmission among the nodes, known as Medium Access Protocol (MAC Protocol). If a link is connecting only one sender node and one receiver node, i.e., point-to-point connection; in this case, the MAC protocol is very simple, i.e., a frame can be transmitted when the link is idle.

Reliable Delivery: A link layer protocol may provide reliable delivery of network datagram by using the acknowledgment and retransmission mechanism. For low-bit error links, for example, fiber optic, coaxial, and twisted pair cables, the implementation of reliable delivery at data link layer is a burden because reliable transport service is also provided at the transport layer. However, if a link has a high error rate, such as a wireless link, then reliable delivery at data link layer is required.

Detection and Correction of Error: When a frame is transmitted at the sender node into the physical link, it might be possible that frame bits may be changed in the link due to signal attenuation and electromagnetic noise. Therefore, at the receiver node, there is a possibility that it receives incorrect data. Therefore, a mechanism is also implemented at the link layer for the detection & correction of bit errors in the frame. Usually, hardware implementation is preferred for error detection at the data link layer.

2.3.1 Data Link Layer Implementation

Most parts of the data link layer services are implemented in hardware. These services are mainly, accessing link or detecting bits error. This hardware is called a network adapter or network interface card (NIC). For example, Intel's 700 Series adapter implements Ethernet protocol. The IEEE 802.11 WiFi protocol is implemented on Atheros AR5006 controller. Some parts of (such as inserting link-layer address information into the frame and activating network adapter controller hardware) the link layer protocol is implemented as program (i.e., software). This executes on the CPU of the system which implements it. The data link layer protocol (software implemented portion), at the sender node, takes network datagram from upper (network) layer, which is stored in the memory and creates a frame by inserting the address information and control information. After creating a frame, it activates the network adapter controller, which takes the frame and transmits it to the physical link. On the receiver's node, the network adapter controller receives the frame. After getting the entire frame, it extracts network datagram from it. Network adapter controller raises interrupts to CPU when it receives a frame. Software implemented portion of the link layer protocol responds to this interrupt and sends the network datagram to the network layer for further processing. The data link layer is a place in the protocol stack where software and hardware meet.

2.3.2 Link Layer Addressing

A network interface adapter has an address called the link-layer address, commonly known as a physical address, LAN address, or MAC address. A host/end system or router may have multiple network interface adapters. Each network adapter of the device has a link-layer address. The physical address size is 6 bytes for LAN technology, such as Ethernet and IEEE 802.11 wireless LAN. No network adapter can have the same physical address as others. Physical address space is managed by IEEE.

Address Resolution Protocol (ARP): The address resolution protocol maps the IP address to the MAC address. To understand how the ARP works, consider an example in which 6 nodes are connected, as shown in **Figure 2.7**. Suppose that host A wishes to transmit a network packet to host C, then host A creates a frame by the network packet, including the destination MAC address of host C. In the network packet, the destination IP addresses are already there. But how the network adapter finds the MAC address of host C. So here, address resolution protocol comes into the scene. An ARP table is maintained by each host/router. The question is how this ARP table is built from empty. Suppose the MAC address of host **C** is not in the ARP table of host A. Host A will create an ARP request packet that contains A's IP address, A's MAC address, and C's IP address and MAC broadcast address (FF:FF:FF:FF:FF:FF). Host A sends this ARP request packet in the subnet **P**. ARP request packet is received by all the hosts in the subnet **P**. All the host check if the destination IP address is equal to its own IP address, then it creates an ARP response packet and puts its MAC address and sends it directly to the sender host A. Host A updates its ARP table. After getting the host C MAC address, it creates a frame and sends it to host C. An ARP table entry has a time to live field, i.e., a MAC address entry is deleted after some time (usually, it is 20 minutes).

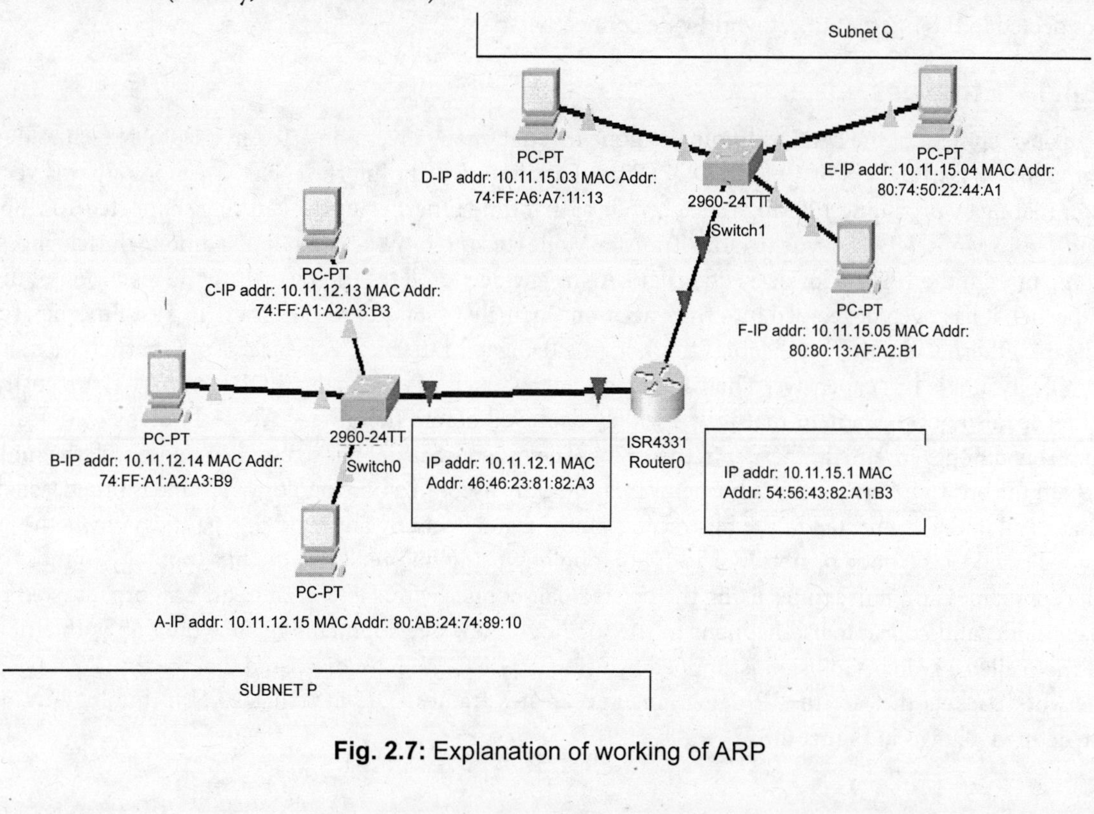

Fig. 2.7: Explanation of working of ARP

Suppose host **A** wishes to transmit a packet to host E, which is in a different subnet. The sending host A passes the network packet, i.e., IP datagram, to its network adapter. To send a network packet from subnet **P** to a host in subnet **Q**, the network packet must be transmitted to the router interface. Thus, here the destination MAC address for the frame would be the MAC address of the router interface, namely 46:46:23:81:82:A3. (The sender host **A** cannot directly use the MAC address of host E in the frame as a destination MAC address. If it uses, then all the frames from host A are sent in subnet **P**, but there is no network adapter of that address, and the frame will be discarded by everyone.) The network adapter at the router receives the frame and sees that if it is addressed for it, then it passes to the network layer of the router. Now router finds the appropriate interface by its forwarding table and passes it to the network interface adapter. Now, here a frame is created with the MAC address of host **E** (obtained using ARP).

2.4 LOCAL AREA NETWORK

When you want to make a computer network for a building, school campus, university campus, or small industry, we connect the end system with network connecting devices with the help of transmission links. A network which is spanned in a small geographical area is termed a local area network. This network can be built using a wired medium or wireless medium, or a mixture of both mediums. So, it is generally wired LAN or wireless LAN. This chapter describes Ethernet LAN technology, which is a wired LAN. This chapter discusses the IEEE 802.11 Wireless LAN (people commonly known it as WiFi) and Bluetooth LAN (Both are wireless local area networks). The local area network can be used as a standalone network for communication and other network-based services. Generally, all LANs are connected to the Internet to get worldwide connectivity.

2.4.1 Ethernet

The development of the LAN technologies gone through many inventions. Token ring LAN technology came in 1984. In the era of 1990s, FDDI (Fiber Distributed Data Interface) LAN technology was very dominating by providing 100Mbps speed while at that time Ethernet and Token ring supported 10Mbps and 4 to 16 Mbps. ATM (Asynchronous Transfer Mode) technology became popular among the telephone companies in the 1990s. However, Ethernet LAN is a widely used technology. Since the invention of the Ethernet, it has been developed into five variations, namely (a) Standard Ethernet, (b) Fast Ethernet, (c) Gigabit Ethernet, and (d) 10 Gigabit Ethernet, (e) 40 Gigabit Ethernet. The success of Ethernet lies in its simplicity and is less expensive. The LAN technologies, such as token ring, FDDI, and ATM are costly. Ethernet also got the benefit that it was widely deployed before the other LAN technologies. Metcalfe and David Boggs invented Ethernet in the 1970s. They used a coaxial bus to connect nodes. Till the mid-1990s, the bus topology for the Ethernet was commonly used. In a bus topology, a frame is broadcasted; that is, all nodes connected to the bus receive all the frames sent by any sender, regardless of whether it is dedicated to the node or not. By late 1990, topology using hub replaced the bus topology in most of the companies and universities using the twisted pair copper wire. Here, frames are still broadcasted to each node, and collision also happens in the topology. New developments replace the hub with a new device called a switch. Collision is stopped by using a switch. We have discussed that the link layer takes network packets that are the IP datagrams and creates frames. The Ethernet LAN technology frame structure is shown in **Figure 2.8.**

Preamble 7 bytes (10101010 10101010 10101010 10101010 10101010 10101010 10101010)	Start Frame Delimiter 1 byte (10101011)	Destination Physical Address 6 bytes	Source Physical Address 6 bytes	Types 2 bytes	Data along with padding min 46 bytes to max 1500 bytes	Cyclic Redundancy Check 4 bytes

Fig. 2.8: Ethernet frame

The sender host's network adapter encapsulates the IP datagram by adding the information header and CRC. This Ethernet frame is passed to the physical layer for transmission. The description of the frame is given below.

Preamble and Start Frame Delimiter: The objective of the preamble is to wake up and synchronize the receivers' network adapter to receive frame. It is 8 bytes. The first 7 bytes are 10101010 10101010 10101010 10101010 10101010 10101010 10101010, and the last byte is 10101011. Start frame delimiter is the 8th byte. The objective of this is to indicate to receiver that the frame is going to start.

Destination Physical Address: This is MAC address, i.e., physical address of the destination host's network adapter. It is 6 bytes. Destination physical address field in the Ethernet frame could either be the physical address of the destination host's network adapter or could be broadcast physical address.

Source Physical Address: This field contains the sender host's network adapter MAC address. It is 6 bytes.

Type: It is a 2 bytes field. This is used to distinguish at the receiving end that which network layer protocol is intended for the packet. The host may run network layer protocols, such as IP, NovellIPX, or AppleTalk. For Internet, the IP protocol is used. The frame may be intended for ARP protocol. For the packet intended to ARP, the 'type' field value is 8086 (hexadecimal) in binary 1000 0000 1000 0110.

Data: The IP datagram, i.e., the network packet, is in this field. The minimum size is 46 bytes. It simply means that the smallest size of the IP datagram should not be less than 46 bytes. If it is less, then more stuff would be added to make it 46 bytes. The network layer finds the actual length of the datagram using the length field in the datagram, and the remaining added stuff is dropped, at the receiving node. Ethernet protocol sends maximum 1500 bytes size of a datagram, i.e., maximum transfer unit (MTU) is 1500. If an IP datagram is larger than this, then the IP datagram is fragmented to make it small.

Cyclic Redundancy Check (CRC): This field content is utilised to detect an error in the frame at the receiver node. It is of 4 bytes. As the frame is transmitted on the physical link, it may be corrupted due to some reasons, like attenuation, interference, or malfunction. At the receiving end, the receiver may check whether the received data is the same as it is sent by the sender. It is possible to detect most of bit errors, but there is a chance that they may be undetected because CRC does not guarantee to detect every error.

Ethernet evolved over many years. Different flavors of Ethernet are developed, for example, 10BASE-T, 100BASE-T, 10GBASE-T, and 40GBASE-T. The first part of the name indicates the speed, such as 10 megabits per second, 100 megabits per second, and 10G, i.e., 10 gigabits per second, 40 gigabits per second. 'BASE' indicates the baseband Ethernet. It simply means that the physical medium only transports the Ethernet frame. 'T' indicates the twisted pair of copper wire. The Ethernet standards which use fiber optic cables are 100BASE-FX, 100BASE-SX, and 100BASE-BX. Nowadays, switch-based Ethernet LAN, in which a switch is connected to the network adapter in full duplex (i.e., it can send and receive simultaneously without any collision). There is no collision in switch-based Ethernet.

2.4.2 IEEE 802.11 Wireless LAN

The IEEE 802.11 wireless LAN, also commonly referred to as WiFi, is a local area network installed in the places like universities, coffee houses, bus stops, airports, railway stations, and homes. There are many standards of 802.11 wireless LAN, as shown [Kurose and Ross] in **Table 2.2.** The IEEE 802.11af and IEEE 802.11ah cover a long distance that is up to one kilometer. It is suitable for sensor networks, the Internet of Things, and metering applications, such as smart meters in smart grids. At the physical layers, the IEEE 802.11 LAN operates mainly in two frequency ranges (i) 2.4 GHz to 2.485 GHz, which is termed as 2.4 GHz WiFi range, (ii) 5.1GHz to 5.8 GHz, which is termed as the 5 GHz WiFi range.

Table 2.2: Different versions of 802.11 wireless LAN

Year	IEEE 802.11 Standards	max data rate	range (MEters)	frequency Band
1999	802.11b	11 Mbps	30	2.4 – 2.485 GHz
2003	802.11g	54 Mbps	30	2.4 – 2.485 GHz
2009	802.11n	600 Mbps	70	2.4 – 2.485 GHz and 5.1 – 5.8 GHz
2013	802.11ac	3.47 Gbps	70	5.1 – 5.8 GHz
2014	802.11af	560 Mbps	1000	54 – 790 MHz
2017	802.11ah	347 Mbps	1000	902 - 928 MHz
2020	802.11ax	14 Gbps	70	2.4 – 2.485 GHz and 5.1 – 5.8 GHz

A wireless network consists of (i) wireless host (wireless hosts are devices such as mobile phones, laptops, sensors, tablets, etc.), (ii) wireless link (it is basically the electromagnetic waves, many technologies are developed to establish a communication link with different data rates and distances), (iii) base station (wireless host connects using a wireless link to a base station; a base station is a device which coordinates the transmission of data packets among the wireless hosts), and (iv) network infrastructure.

If a base station is present in a network, it is termed infrastructure mode. If no base station is in the network, that network is termed ad hoc network. In this type of wireless network, the wireless host must do the routing, address assignment, name translation, etc.

A larger network may be Ethernet LAN or Internet to which the wireless hosts want to connect through the wireless access point. A wireless network may be formed in such a way that in which each wireless host is directly connected to a base station (that is, single hop). After that, the base station has connection with a large wired network such as the Internet. Many of the WiFi networks in our universities and classrooms are single hop infrastructure-based networks.

There is another way to form a wireless network in which there is no base station. Bluetooth network is mainly formed to connect a keyboard, mouse speaker, etc. There are other wireless networks formed by different arrangements, namely wireless mesh networks, mobile ad hoc networks, and vehicular ad hoc networks. These are out of the scope of this book.

In the wireless link, electromagnetic radiation attenuates when it passes through objects matters like buildings walls. The electromagnetic waves lose their signal strength as distance increases from a sender device to a receiver device. Electromagnetic wave also suffers from interference with other wave and noise.

Wireless LAN Architecture: The wireless LAN architecture is simply how components in wireless LAN are interconnected. A Basic Service Set (BSS) is a fundamental unit that consists of a central base station (called wireless access point in the jargon of wireless LAN) and wireless hosts/ end systems. BSS further has connection with either a switch or router to make the network larger.

Note: In many cases, the access points (AP) and router are combined as a single device.

In wireless LAN architecture, each wireless station is assigned with a physical address. It is saved in network interface adopter of the wireless station. It is of 6 bytes. The wireless station can be organized into two ways (i) infrastructural mode and (ii) ad hoc mode. In **Figure 2.9**, an infrastructure mode wireless LAN, an access point (AP) is connected to six wireless stations and connected to a switch and further connected to a router. The access point may also have a wired Ethernet interface which can be connected to either a switch or router.

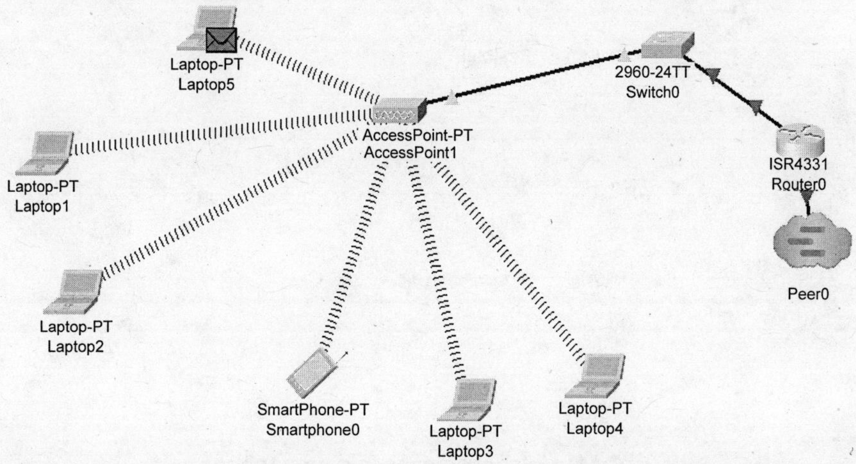

Fig. 2.9: A wireless network – infrastructure mode

As shown in **Figure 2.10**, wireless stations can form a network without any central station named as ad hoc network. It is formed on the fly. It may be formed with laptops or mobile phones in the classroom among the students to share files such as text files or video files, etc. It does not require any centralized access point.

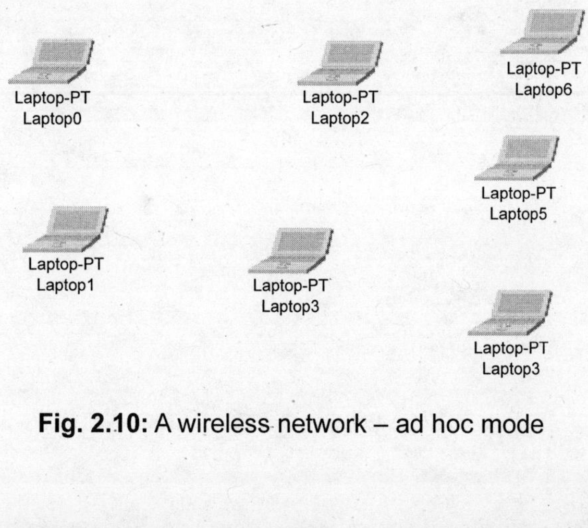

Fig. 2.10: A wireless network – ad hoc mode

In infrastructure wireless LAN, an access point has a Service Set Identifier (SSID) that is assigned by the person (administrator) who is installing the wireless LAN. As shown in **Figure 2.11,** if you open your smartphone hotspot setting, you can see the SSID field, here RealMeB, security, and password field, here you can set a password for your hotspot. You can also see the 'SELECT APBAND' field, which is set to a 2.4GHz band. Your smartphone hotspot acts as a wireless access point (WAP), which provides Internet to the connected devices. On the other hand, when you open the WiFi of your phone, you will see the SSID of the available access point in the range, as shown in **Figure 2.12.** These SSIDs are EMP, GUEST, STUD, and TechzoneW/H_2.4G.

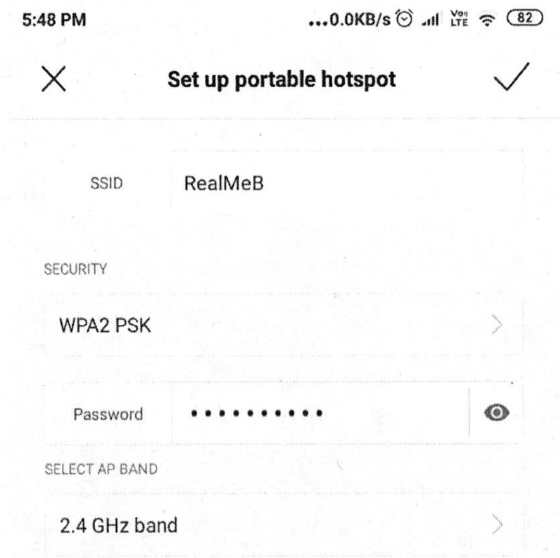

Fig. 2.11: Hotspot settings in a smartphone

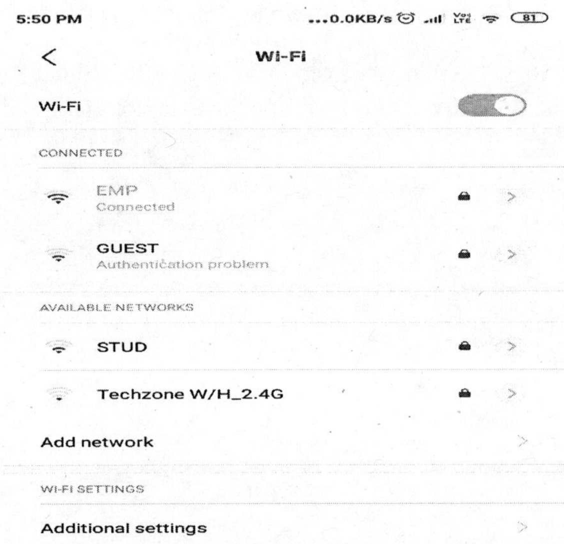

Fig. 2.12: Available APs SSID for a Wi-Fi

As we have seen that the IEEE 802.11 standards operates mostly in frequency band 2.4 GHz to 2.4835 GHz, the frequency band is 2.4835 GHz - 2.4 GHz = 83.5 MHz. This band is divided into overlapping channels. Suppose you want to connect a wireless device to an access point. The question is how your device will know there is an access point out there. To solve this issue, an access point sends a frame containing SSID and MAC address of the AP periodically. This frame is known as **beacon frame**. So, your wireless device will scan all 11 channels to get a beacon frame. After getting the information about the AP, your device selects one of the access points to get associated. Passive scanning is defined as when a wireless device scans and listens for beacon frames. On the other hand, in active scanning, a probe frame is broadcasted to all the access points within the range by the wireless station. After receiving the probe frame, the access point responds and sends response frame to the wireless station.

After getting and selecting an access point, the wireless station will be associated with the access point. An association is done by sending and receiving association request and response frame to/from the AP. An association may require authentication. So, the access point communicates with an authentication server, which verifies username and password. The wireless device, after being associated with the AP, obtains an IP address by sending a DHCP (dynamic host configuration protocol) message. After getting an IP address, it can send/receive messages to/from a host in the network.

2.4.3 Bluetooth

Bluetooth technology is used to create a wireless personal area network, also referred to as piconet. It implements the IEEE 802.15 standards protocol. This technology has applications like connecting a wireless headphone, mouse, or keyboard to your computer. It is used to connect a smartwatch or health-monitoring device to a smartphone. A Bluetooth network spans an area of radius about 10 meters. It works at low power. The Bluetooth device works at a 2.4 GHz radio band and is prone to have interfered with the other electromagnetic wave. The data rate by a Bluetooth device can be achieved up to 3 Mbps. A piconet network is an ad-hoc network that supports generally maximum 8 devices at a time. One device acts as primary (i.e., master), and the remaining seven devices act as secondary nodes. Bluetooth technology uses mechanisms such as time division multiplexing, randomized backoff, error detection, and acknowledgment for the reliable transfer of data.

2.5 SWITCHING TECHNIQUE

In a network of computers, data moves from one place to another through transmission links and switches. Two fundamental ways to transmit data are (i) circuit switching and (ii) packet switching.

2.5.1 Circuit Switching

Circuit switching requires reserving the resources along the path between communicating entities for entire duration of the session. A path is to be established which is dedicated for the sending host and receiving host for the entire period of the communication session before the transmission. This is called a circuit in the field of telephony. It has three stages (i) circuit (path) establishment, (ii) data transmission, and (iii) circuit path termination. Circuit switching is inefficient; however, it can transmit data at a guaranteed constant rate.

2.5.2 Packet Switching

In this type of transmission, a long message is broken into small chunks, referred to as a packet. A network is constituted of end systems, transmission links, and packet switches. A packet switch generally receives the entire packet at its input link, after that, forward to the outgoing link based on some criteria which led the packet to its destination. This process is commonly named store and forward packet switching. A router (a packet switch that is working up to the network layer) processes the packet before forwarding it to the outgoing link interface. Each packet switch has many links on which packets arrive. There is a buffer (called queue) associated with each link. When a packet comes at a link and it is supposed to be forwarded through an outgoing link, it can only be transmitted through the outgoing link if it is not busy; if the outgoing link is busy in sending some other packet, then this packet will wait in the buffer termed queue (this waiting time is called queuing delay). If the queue has not space, that is full, packet loss happens because it is dropped. Circuit switched networking companies are adapting packet switched networking due to its benefits.

UNIT SUMMARY

This unit describes different types of the transmission medium and their characteristics. These mediums are classified into two categories, namely wired and wireless. Wired mediums such as fiber optical cable, coaxial, and twisted pair cable are discussed. The frequency band of the electromagnetic spectrum, which is used in telecommunication, is discussed. Different types of topologies, such as bus, tree, and star, are elucidated so that one can create a local area network. Data link layer, Ethernet, WiFi, Bluetooth, and switching techniques are discussed, by which a learner understands the working of a local area network. Along with this, data center networking is discussed to get more insight.

EXERCISES

Multiple Choice Questions

1. Which of the following cable is twisted and have insulated copper wire?
   (a) Fiber optic (b) twisted pair (c) coaxial (d) all
2. Which of the following cable is constructed using glass or plastic as a core?
   (a) Fiber optic (b) Coaxial (c) Twisted pair (d) all
3. What layer of the OSI model talks about the transmission media?
   (a) Application Layer (b) Network Layer
   (c) Physical Layer (d) Presentation Layer
4. Pulse of light is transmitted for data transmission in which of the following medium?
   (a) Copper cable (b) Unshielded twisted pair
   (c) Coaxial cable (d) Fiber optic cable
5. In a transmission medium, attenuation refers to?
   (a) Loss of energy or strength of signal (b) addition of more unwanted signal
   (c) noise (d) none

6. Signal impairment in the transmission medium is?
   (a) noise (b) distortion (c) attenuation (d) all
7. What is the information included in a frame header?
   (a) physical addresses (b) preamble
   (c) CRC (d) all
8. From the protocols given in the options, which one does not belong to data link protocol?
   (a) FTP (b) Ethernet
   (c) Point-to-Point Protocol (d) High Level Data Link Control (HDLC)
9. Data link layer takes a packet from which layer to create a frame?
   (a) Application Layer (b) Transport Layer
   (c) Network Layer (d) Session Layer
10. What is the byte size of the Physical address or MAC address?
   (a) 1 (b) 6 (c) 5 (d) 2

ANSWERS															
1.	(b)	2.	(a)	3.	(c)	4.	(d)	5.	(a)	6.	(d)	7.	(d)	8.	(a)
9.	(c)	10.	(b)												

Questions (Short Answers)

1. What is the role of a transmission medium?
2. Differentiate between the wired and wireless medium?
3. Write the frequency bands which are used in wireless local area networks?
4. Differentiate between twisted pair, coaxial, and fiber optic cables?
5. What is the purpose of twisting the cable in a wired medium?
6. What is Ethernet protocol?
7. What is the purpose of a physical address (i.e., MAC Address)?
8. What is the purpose of a network interface card?
9. What is the difference between circuit switching and packet switching?
10. Write a short note on Bluetooth?

Questions (Long Answer)

1. Describe the working of the Address Resolution Protocol.
2. Describe the data link layer tasks and challenges.
3. Explain the working of Ethernet technology and its frame format.
4. Explain the working of wireless LAN (WiFi).

PRACTICALS

Aim - 1

Examination of cables of various companies on Internet and write the specifications of those cables. Examine the different connectors on Internet and write about that.

Aim -2

Creation of patch cords using cables and connectors of different types of wired medium. Figure 2.13 shows twisted pair cable, RJ-45 connector, tester, crimping, and splicing tools.

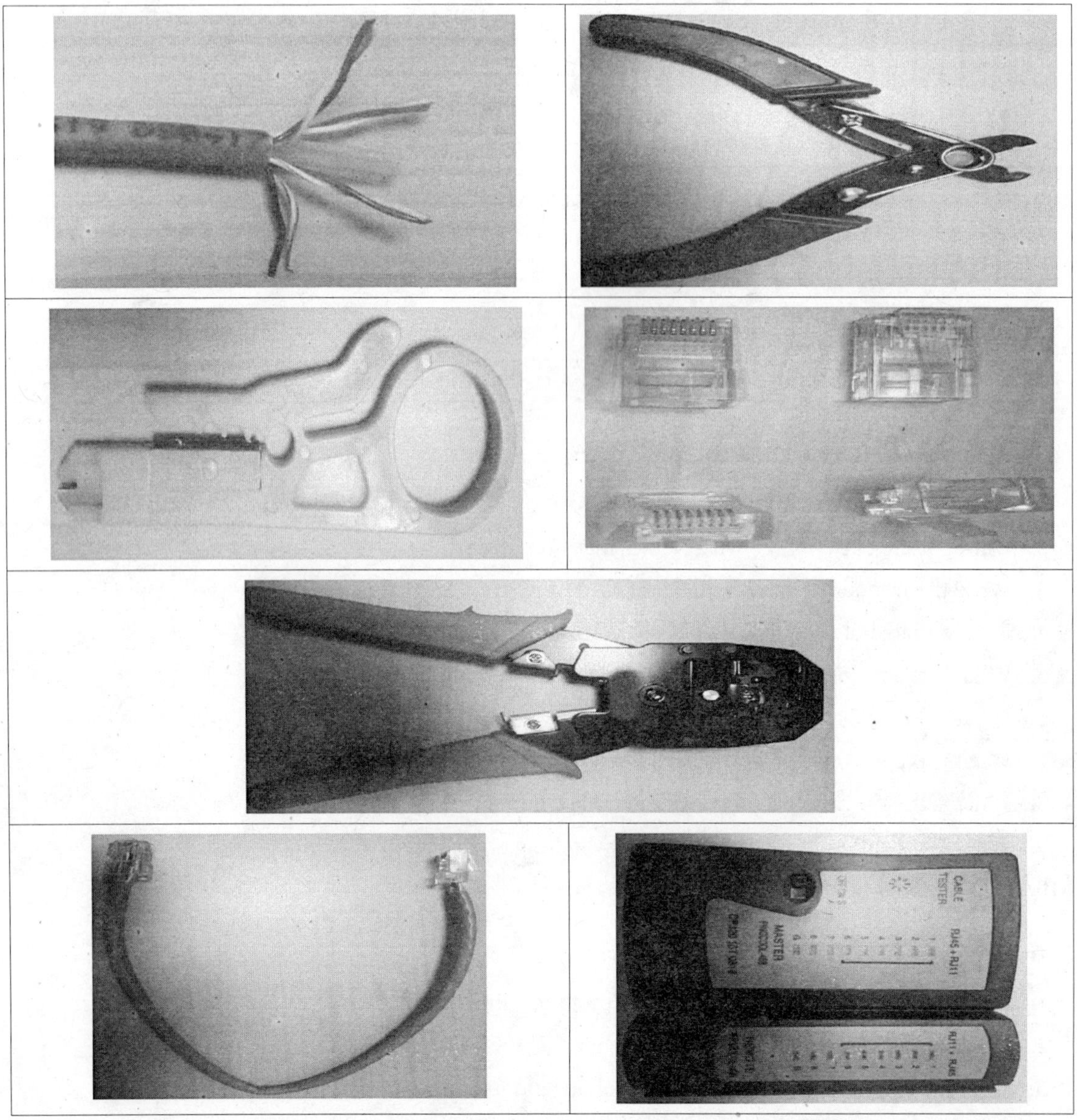

Fig. 2.13: RJ-45 Connector, Twisted Pair Cable, and Tools

KNOW MORE

Data Center Network

Companies like Google, Amazon.com, Alibaba, and Microsoft have built data centers that have 10,000 to 1,00,000 hosts. These hosts are interconnected, which makes a data center network. The objective of these data centers is to provide services, such as web pages, searching, email, and video, to provide a very large computing infrastructure, and to provide cloud computing service. The cost of a large data center having 1,00,000 hosts is more than $12,000,000 per month. In which, 15% of the cost is associated with networking [Kurose and Ross]. A host generally has a CPU, memory, and hard disk, commonly called a blade. A rack contains approximately 20 to 40 blades. A switch is associated with each blade and put on the top of the rack, known as top of rack switch. A blade in a data center typically has very high-speed Ethernet, such as 40 Gbps or 100 Gbps. Each host has an IP address. All the rack switches have connected to other rack switches using switches in a hierarchical fashion or highly connected to one another to make a data center network. Generally, companies do not disclose their connection strategy.

REFERENCES AND SUGGESTED READINGS

1. Andrew S. Tanenbaum, Computer Networks, 5th Edition, PHI
2. W. Richard Stevens, TCP/IP Illustrated, Volume-1, Addision Wesley, Second Edition
3. James F. Kurose and Keith W. Ross, Computer Networking: A Top–Down Approach, Pearson, Eight Edition
4. Behrouz A. Forouzan and Firouz Mosharraf, Computer Networks: A Top-Down Approach, Mc Graw Hill Education, Special Indian Edition 2012
5. William Stalling, Computer Networking with Internet Protocols and Technology, Pearson Education, First Edition

Dynamic QR Code for Further Reading

❑❑

3 Network Layer, Routing Algorithms, and Protocols

UNIT SPECIFICS

Through this unit, we discuss the following aspects:

- Network layer;
- IP protocol version 4 and addressing;
- Routing principles;
- Distance vector routing;
- Link state routing;
- OSPF protocol;
- RIP protocol.

This unit explains the network layer, internet protocol version 4, addressing, routing principles, distance vector routing, link state routing, OSPF, and RIP protocol. A network layer is a place from where different networks can be connected to make one large network. Its purpose is to transport a datagram from one end system to another end system. That is, an end system to end system delivery is performed by the network layer. This unit contains questions for practice. This also provides references for further reading. There is a "Know More" section carefully designed that gives supplementary information based on the context of this unit. A laboratory task is included to get acquainted with the configurations of devices to make a network.

RATIONALE

This unit on the network layer helps students to get an understanding of how a datagram is transported, how a route is determined, how different algorithms and protocols are implemented for route finding, and how an address is assigned to an end system and router. All these aspects are relevant to understand the working of a computer network.

PRE-REQUISITES

This unit requires unit 1 & 2.

UNIT OUTCOMES

List of outcomes of this unit is given below:

U3-O1: Description of the network layer

U3-O2: Describe internet protocol

U3-O3: Explain IP addressing and routing

U3-O4: Understand the routing algorithm

U3-O5: Understand routing protocol

Unit-3 Outcomes	EXPECTED MAPPING WITH COURSE OUTCOMES (1- Weak Correlation; 2- Medium correlation; 3- Strong Correlation)				
	CO-1	CO-2	CO-3	CO-4	CO-5
U3-O1	2	2	3	3	3
U3-O2	3	3	3	3	3
U3-O3	3	3	3	3	3
U3-O4	2	2	2	3	3
U3-O5	2	3	2	2	2

3.1 NETWORK LAYER

Network layer protocol provides host-to-host (i.e., end system to end system) packet delivery. Network layer protocol executes on end systems and routers. Remember, the application layer protocol and transport layer protocol execute on end systems, that is, hosts only. The tasks of the network layer are implemented in two parts (i) data plane and (ii) control plane. The goal of this layer protocol is to move datagram packets (that is, network layer packet, also known as datagram) from a source host to the destination host.

Forwarding: A router performs the forwarding of a packet. A router is a device in which the network layer protocol is running. Router receives datagram packet at its input link and forwards these datagram packets by looking forwarding table to appropriate output link. The forwarding of packets is implemented in the data plane. Forwarding simply means transmitting a packet from the router's input link to the router's appropriate output link. A forwarding mechanism is generally implemented in hardware and typically takes a **few nanoseconds.**

Routing: There can be multiple routers which are making a path from a source host to a destination host. The network layer finds a path or route for a packet through which the packet flows. An algorithm that finds a path is known as a routing algorithm. Routing algorithms are implemented in the control plane. Routing simply means finding a path between a source host to a destination host, termed an end-to-end path. It is a network-wide task. Routing takes more significant time, typically a **few milliseconds to seconds**. Routing protocols are generally implemented in software.

A router forwards a packet by looking into its forwarding table. The question arises of how this forwarding table is constructed. A routing algorithm decides the contents of a forwarding table. In the traditional approach, the routing algorithm executes at each router and computes the values for the forwarding table. A routing algorithm (implemented as a program/process) running in a router needs to communicate with the routing algorithm process running in another router to fill the information in its forwarding table. This communication is done by exchanging messages among routers. In the software defined network approach, a remote controller executes the routing algorithm functionalities and sends the forwarding table to all the routers. In this case, a router only performs the forwarding by looking at its forwarding table. The implementation of a remote controller may be at a data center, or may be at an ISP.

TCP/IP protocol stack's Internet layer implements a best-effort delivery service. Best-effort delivery service does not guarantee in-order delivery, that is, the order in which the packets were transmitted at the source may be delivered or may not be delivered in the same order at the destination. It also does not guarantee of delivery of the packet, which means unreliable. Error control is not implemented in the network layer in TCP/IP model; however, the network layer implements a mechanism to detect the error in the datagram header by using a checksum field. An auxiliary protocol ICMP is also implemented, which provides information when a datagram is discarded. In TCP/IP model, the Internet layer does not implement flow control. Congestion control is also not implemented by the network layer (i.e., Internet layer) in TCP/IP model. Congestion is a situation when there are too many datagrams in the network which are above the network capacity. Therefore, datagrams are dropped by routers.

Let us look inside a router to understand the network layer protocol working. Unit – 5 of this book gives more working details of a router. An abstract view of a router is depicted in **Figure 3.1.** A router has a processor that executes the routing algorithm, manages the routing table, and executes network management functions. The switching fabric of a router connects the input port to the output port. At the input port, the forwarding table is consulted to determine the output port. A packet carrying the routing protocol information, known as a control packet, is forwarded to the router's processor. A packet, which is received by the switch fabric, is restored in the outgoing buffer (queue) by the output port (interface) and transmitted to outgoing link. At the output port, the required link layer and physical layer functions are performed to transmit a packet. The input port, switch fabric, and output port are almost implemented in the hardware.

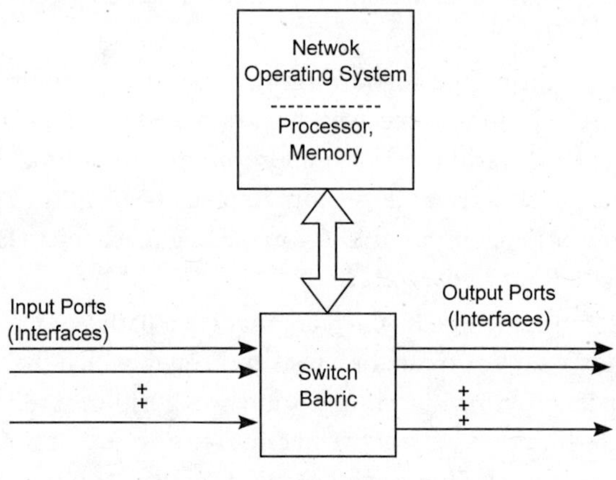

Fig. 3.1: An abstract view of a router

3.1.1 Network Performance

A network is an infrastructure for the transportation of a message. In a packet-switched network, a message is divided into packets. Network service (i.e., transportation of a packet from one place to another place) is used by the upper layer protocols. A network performance is measured by parameters, such as packet loss, throughput, and delay.

Packet Loss: A network consists of transmission links, switches, and routers. A router has a memory buffer (called input queue and output queue) to hold a packet. This memory is finite (i.e., limited). When a router receives a packet at its input port, and the input queue is full, then the packet is (omitted) dropped. That is, a packet is transmitted into the network, but it is lost. Therefore, the packet is retransmitted into the network, which may lead to an overflow of the network and result in more packet loss.

Throughput: Throughput is described as the transmission of data bits per second at a point. Let say, host **X** sends data to host **Y.** At Y, the throughput is the instantaneous data rate at which Y receives a file. Look at the scenario in **Figure 3.2**, the throughput is 10Mbps (the lowest).

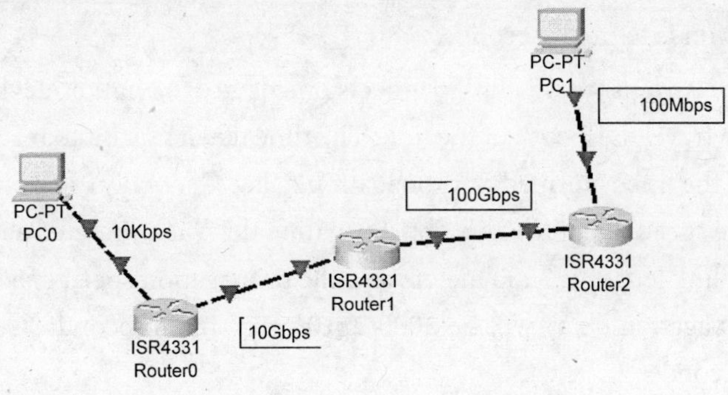

Fig. 3.2: A network scenario 1

Another scenario to calculate throughput is given in Figure 3.3. Here the link (1000Kbps) is shared by four computers on one side and by four computers on another side. Suppose the PC 4, 5, 6, and 7 are downloading files from PC 0, 1, 2, and 3 simultaneously. Therefore, the throughput is 1000/4= 250Kbps.

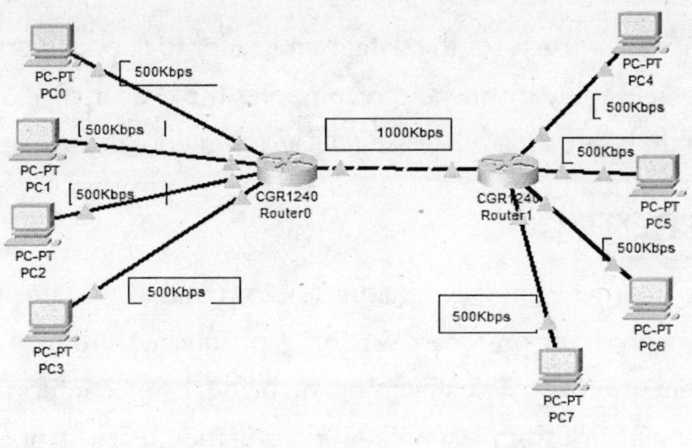

Fig. 3.3: A network scenario 2

Delay: When a source sends a packet to a destination through a network, it takes some times to be delivered. This time is termed as a delay. A network is built by using end systems, transmission links, switches, and routers. Different kinds of delays occurred at a different portion of the network. These delays are namely, transmission, propagation, queueing, and processing delay. The total delay is the addition of all these delays.

Transmission Delay: A device is connected through a transmission link. When the device sends a packet, it puts the packet on the link bit by bit. For example, suppose a packet size is p bits. Transmission delay is the time difference between the time (say t_1) at which the first bit of packet is put on the link and the time (say t_p) at which last bit of the packet is out on the link. The transmission delay is $t_p - t_1$. It depends on the speed of the transmission link. Suppose the link transmission speed is d bits per second. The transmission delay is calculated as packet size/transmission speed, i.e., p/d seconds. For example, if size of a packet is 15000 bits and transmission speed is 150000000 bits per second, the transmission delay will be 15000/150000000 seconds, i.e., 0.0001 seconds or 100 microseconds. Typically, transmission delay is of order milliseconds to microseconds.

Propagation Delay: A transmission link connects one device to another device. It may be wired or wireless. A packet has to travel the length of the link. The time taken by a bit to reach from one end of the link to the other end of the link is termed as propagation delay. Generally, the propagation speed of the medium is similar to the speed of light. Value of propagation delay is computed as distance/propagation speed. For example, if a link length is 3000 meters and the propagation speed of a bit in the link is $2x10^8$ meters/second, the propagation delay will be $3000/2x10^8$ = 15 microseconds. Generally, it is of order milliseconds to microseconds.

Queuing Delay: As we have seen, a router receives a packet from its input port and forwards it to the output port. A packet may have to wait in the input and output queue (i.e., buffer) due to the routing processor may be busy processing another packet or the output link is busy transmitting some other packet. This waiting time in the queue is termed a queuing delay. In practice, it is an order of microseconds to milliseconds.

Processing Delay: A router processes the datagram header to check an error in the header. It also decreases the time to live field value by one and recomputes the header checksum. The time taken for the processing of a datagram is termed a processing delay. In practice, it is an order of microseconds.

3.2 INTERNET PROTOCOL

There are two versions of Internet Protocol (version 4 and version 6) which is used in today's Internet. Internet protocol is a network layer protocol. Version 4 of Internet Protocol is written as IPv4. It is a connectionless datagram protocol. The meaning of being connectionless is that each packet is independently sent in the network from a source to a destination. Packets of a single message may be transmitted through different routes and may be delivered out of order. A packet of network layer is termed as a datagram.

IPv4 Datagram Format: Generally, a datagram is made from a transport layer protocol packet (i.e., segment), either a TCP packet or UDP packet, in the case of the Internet. However, it may be made for another type of message, such as ICMP data. **Figure 3.4**. shows IPv4 datagram structure. The description of fields of the format are given below.

<table>
<tr><td>Version
(4 bits)</td><td>Header Length
(4 bits)</td><td>Type of Service
(8 bits)</td><td colspan="3">Datagram Length (16 bits)</td></tr>
<tr><td colspan="3">Identification (16 bits)</td><td>Flags (3 bits)</td><td colspan="2">Fragmentation Offset
(13 bits)</td></tr>
<tr><td colspan="2">Time-to-Live (8 bits)</td><td>Protocol (bits)</td><td></td><td></td><td></td></tr>
<tr><td colspan="6">IP Address (4 bytes or 32 bits) of Source Node</td></tr>
<tr><td colspan="6">IP Address (4 bytes or 32 bits) of Destination Node</td></tr>
<tr><td colspan="6">Options (If any, upto 40 bytes)</td></tr>
<tr><td colspan="6">Data (Payload)</td></tr>
</table>

Fig. 3.4: Internet protocol version 4 datagram format

Version: The version number is necessary for a router or host to know how to interpret the datagram. The 4 bits are used to represent the version number.

Header Length: The IPv4 datagram contains an options field that may be included or may not be included in the datagram according to the need. Therefore, the size of the IPv4 datagram header is variable. To determine where the data (that is, the payload, the packet from the transport layer) begins, the header length is required. Four bits are used to represent the header length. The header length is represented in 4 bytes words. For example, if the value is 1101 that is 13 in decimal, it means the header length is 4 x 13 = 52 bytes. **20 bytes** is the minimum header length, and **60 bytes** is the maximum header length.

Types of Service: Eight bits are used to represent a type of service in this field. The objective of this field is to distinguish the different types of IP datagrams. For instance, it may be used to differentiate real-time application packets from non-real time application packets.

Datagram Length: Sixteen bits are used to represent the datagram length (header and payload). It represents the total length of the IP datagram. The maximum size of the datagram can be **65535 bytes** (that can be represented by 16 bits binary number). However, in practice, usually the datagram size is 1500 bytes, which fits in the maximum payload size of the Ethernet frame.

Identification, Flags, and Fragmentation Offset: Fragmentation of an IP datagram uses these fields. There may be a situation where a large IP datagram is fragmented and transmitted to the destination host independently. At the destination, the Internet Protocol reassembles and then forwards to the transport layer. In the new version IPv6, fragmentation is not allowed.

Time-to-Live: Eight bits are used to represent the time-to-live field. The objective of the time-to-live value is to stop a datagram from circulating in the network forever. At every router, this value is decremented by one. If it is zero, the router drops it.

Protocol: Eight bits are used to represent this field. This field is used at the destination node. The Internet protocol needs to find out which protocol, for example, TCP, UDP, ICMP, IGMP, or OSPF. This field value for ICMP is 1, for IGMP is 2, for TCP is 6, for UDP is 17, and for OSPF is 89.

Header Checksum: An error in an IP header creates a problem. For instance, if the destination address is erroneous, then the datagram will not be delivered to the right/correct node. If the protocol field is erroneous, the datagram will not be delivered to the right/correct protocol of the upper layer. If the fragmentation fields are erroneous, reassembling of the datagram is not possible. If the total datagram length field is erroneous, it will consider more or less size of the payload, and so on. One important point is that the header checksum is recalculated at every router, and it is stored in the datagram header because at each router time-to-leave field is changed as it is decremented by one at each router.

Source and Destination IP Address of Node: 32 bits IP address of a source node and 32 bits IP address of a destination node are stored in this field. At a sender host, the sender puts its own IP address. The IP address of the destination host may be found by (DNS) Domain Name System and be placed in the datagram.

Options: The options field is up to 40 bytes in size. The option fields allow IP header extension. It is used for network testing and debugging.

Payload (Data): Payload is the packet from the protocol, for example, TCP, UDP, ICMP, etc., which uses the service of the IP protocol.

3.3 IPV4 ADDRESSING

Internet address or IP address is used to identify the devices (specifically end systems and routers) on the Internet. Generally, an end system or host has one interface connected to a network. A router has multiple interfaces. The end system and routers send and receive IP datagrams. Therefore, Internet protocol requires router interfaces and end system interface have unique IP addresses. In a nutshell, generally, an end system has one IP address, and a router has multiple IP addresses. If an end system has two links or connections to the Internet, it will have two IP addresses. Technically, the association of an IP address is with the interface instead of an end system or a router (that contains it).

Internet protocol version 4 uses 32 bits binary number to represent an IP address. The total number of IP addresses that can be formed by a 32 bits binary number is 2^{32}, i.e., approximately 400 crore (4 billion). Dotted decimal notation is used to write an IP address. It is simply each byte is written as a decimal value. For example, 10101100 00011111 10000100 00000010 written as 172.31.132.2.

3.3.1 Classful Addressing

A 32-bit IP address has two parts (i) prefix and (ii) suffix. Prefix is used to determine network, and the suffix is used to determine node within the network. If n bits are used for a prefix, then the remaining (32-n) bits are used for the suffix. In classful addressing, a prefix has a fixed length. ***The classful addressing is not generally in use.***

In the classful addressing scheme, 2^{32} (approximately 400 crores) addresses are partitioned into 5 classes, namely, A, B, C, D, and E. The class A, B, and C have prefix 8, 16, and 24 bits, respectively. Class D and E addresses are not broken into prefix and suffix. Class A address is determined by looking first bit (most significant bit or first bit of the first byte or octet) of 32 bits. If it is '0', then it is class A, and the remaining 7 bits are used for network identification. That means $2^7 = 128$ different networks, each of 2^{24} host addresses (two of these addresses are used for special purposes; specifically the first is for network number, and the last is for broadcast), can be formed. It means that these networks are very large network having too many hosts. Class B address is identified by looking the first bit and second bit as '10'. The remaining 14 bits are used for network. Therefore, $2^{14} = 16384$ networks, each network having $2^{16} = 65536$ host addresses (2 of them are used for special purposes), can be formed. Class C address is identified by looking first bit, second bit, and third bit as '110'. The remaining 21 bits are for network. Therefore, $2^{21} = 2097152$ networks, each network with $2^8 = 256$ addresses for hosts (two of them for special purposes), can be formed. Class D address is identified by looking first four bits, it is 1110. It is not partitioned into prefix and suffix. These addresses are used for multicast address. Class E address is identified by looking first four bits, it is 1111. Addresses of Class E are reserved.

Class A Address:

8 bits	8 bits	8 bits	8 bits
prefix	suffix		
0bbb bbbb (first bit 0)	bbbb bbbb	bbbb bbbb	bbbb bbbb
Address range first octet in decimal 0 - 127			'b' is representing either '0' or '1'

Class B Address:

8 bits	8 bits	8 bits	8 bits
prefix		suffix	
10bb bbbb	bbbb bbbb	bbbb bbbb	bbbb bbbb
Address range first octet in decimal 128 - 191			

Class C Address:

8 bits	8 bits	8 bits	8 bits
prefix			suffix
110b bbbb	bbbb bbbb	bbbb bbbb	bbbb bbbb
Address range first octet in decimal 192- 223			

Class D Address:

8 bits	8 bits	8 bits	8 bits
1110 bbbb	bbbb bbbb	bbbb bbbb	bbbb bbbb
Address range first octet in decimal 224 - 239			

Class E Address:

8 bits	8 bits	8 bits	8 bits
1111 bbbb	bbbb bbbb	bbbb bbbb	bbbb bbbb
Address range first octet in decimal 240 - 255			

The classful addresses (2^{32} addresses) are divided as follows

<table>
<tr><td rowspan="3">A – 50%</td><td colspan="2">B – 25%</td></tr>
<tr><td rowspan="2">C – 12.5%</td><td>D – 6.25%</td></tr>
<tr><td>E – 6.25%</td></tr>
</table>

The classification of the addresses as above is not able to fulfill the demand. The growing number of organizations in the world that have small and medium number of end systems in their organization, required more number of networks. The addresses in classful scheme are not distributed efficiently. Many addresses are wasted because very big availability of addresses, but the number of networks is less. Many small organizations were not able to get addresses. This is called address depletion. That is why the classful address scheme is obsolete.

3.3.2 Classless Addressing

To resolve the shortage of IP addresses, a long-term solution is IP version 6 address. However, a short-term solution is also developed by using the same 32 bits. In this, the distribution of addresses is changed, termed as classless addressing. In classless addressing, the addresses are divided into blocks. A block can have 1, 2, 4, ... addresses (i.e., 2^0, 2^1, 2^2, 2^3, 2^4, ...). The restriction is that each block will have addresses in power of 2. The prefix in this addressing scheme is variable. This prefix length is from 0 to 32. If a prefix is small, it means the network has many hosts, i.e., a large network. If a prefix is large, it means the network is small, i.e., it has less number of hosts.

Note: In classless addressing also, the IP address is 4 bytes and is written in dotted decimal notation.

In classless addressing, a prefix is written after the address, separated by a slash (/). For example, 172.16.31.124/25, where 25 is a prefix. This way of writing is called Classless Inter-Domain Routing (CIDR) notation. By a given address, we can find out the first address, last address, and the number of addresses in that block. To find the first address, write the address in binary form and write a mask in which the bits equal to the prefix are one (most significant bits), and the remaining is zero. Perform the 'AND' operation; for example, in address 172.16.31.124/25, the prefix is 25. The calculation is shown in **Table 3.1.**

Table 3.1: First address calculation

Address 172.16.31.124	10101100 00010000 00011111 01111100
Mask 255.255.255.128	11111111 11111111 11111111 10000000
Logical AND operation	10101100 00010000 00011111 00000000
172.16.31.0	172 16 31 0

The first address, in the block in which address 172.16.31.124/25 belongs, is 172.16.31.0/25. The number of IP addresses in a given block is calculated by $2^{32\text{-prefix}}$. For the given example, it is $2^{32-25} = 2^7 =$ 128 addresses. To find the last address, write any address in the block and perform logical OR operation with NOT mask. For instance, **Table 3.2** shows the calculation of last address, i.e., 172.16.31.127/25.

Table 3.2: Last address calculation

Address 172.16.31.124	10101100 00010000 00011111 01111100
Mask 255.255.255.128	11111111 11111111 11111111 10000000
NOT mask 0.0.0.127	00000000 00000000 00000000 01111111
Logical OR operation (address OR NOT mask)	10101100 00010000 00011111 01111111
172.16.31.127	172 16 31 127

In nutshell,

An Address 172.16.31.124/25, No. of addresses = 128, First address = 172.16.31.0/25, Last Address = 172.16.31.127/25

We can observe that the address 172.16.31.124/25 is in between the First and Last address. From the first and last address, we can also count that the total addresses are 128, i.e., 172.16.31.0 to 172.16.31.127. The first address of a block is a network address. Routing of a packet to the destination network requires the network address. How a block of address is allocated to an organization, or company, or a university, etc. The Internet Corporation for Assigned Names and Numbers (ICANN) allocates the IP addresses. Generally, it allocates a large block address to Internet Service Provider, or to a large organization.

The block address allocation must follow the rules given below:

1. A block consists of the number of addresses in power of 2. That is, an organization can request a block in which 2^n number of addresses. For example, $128 = 2^7$ addresses or $64 = 2^6$ addresses. The reason is that, if it is not a power of 2, the prefix value will not be an integer. The prefix n is 32 - $\log_2 N$ where N is number of addresses, we want in the block.
2. Block consists of contiguous addresses.
3. The first address of the block must be divisible by the total number of the addresses of the block. For example, 172.16.31.0/25, the first address is 172.16.31.0, its decimal value is 2886737644 is divisible by 128. The block 172.16.31.0/25 has total 128 addresses. The reason behind the divisibility is that the first address needs to be the prefix followed by (32 -n) number of zeros.

A block of address can be further divided into sub-block for the subnetwork, also termed a subnet. A sub-network can be further partitioned into sub-sub-block and so on, to meet the requirement of the organization. Subnet should be designed (i.e., block of address allocation) in such a way that routing of a packet to a network and sub-network does not create a problem. In a subnet also, the number of addresses should be in the power of 2, contiguous, and the first address of the sub-network is divisible by the number of the addresses in the sub-block. The first address, last address, and the total number of addresses in a sub-block are figured out in the same way as for a block. For example, in block 172.16.31.0/25, the total number of addresses in this block is 128. Let say, there are three small organizations, X, Y, and Z, that require 60 addresses, 32 addresses, and 15 addresses, respectively. The 60 is not in the power of 2; hence, the first sub-block will contain 64 addresses, the second sub-block is 32, it is a power of 2, third sub-block will contain 16 because 15 is not a power of 2. The block division is given in **Table 3.3.**

Table 3.3: Address block division into sub-block

Block 172.16.31.0/25		
X	Y	Z
64 addresses Sub block 172.16.31.0/26 First address 172.16.31.0/26 Last address 172.16.31.63/26	32 addresses Sub block 172.16.31.64/27 First address 172.16.31.64/27 Last address 172.16.31.95/27	16 addresses Sub block 172.16.31.96/28 First address 172.16.31.96/28 Last address 172.16.31.111/28

In address aggregation (that is, an address summarization) is combining multiple blocks into one larger block. There are some special addresses given in **Table 3.4**.

Table 3.4: Special purpose addresses

0.0.0.0/32	This host address	It is used in the case when the sender doesn't know its own IP address.
255.255.255.255/32	Limited broadcast address	When a router or an end system wants to send a datagram to all the nodes in a network, the limited broadcast address is used.
127.0.0.0/8	Loopback address	A datagram never goes outside of the host. It is used to test programs on the same host.
10.0.0.0/8, 172.16.0.0/12, 192.168.0.0/16, 169.254.0.0/16	Private addresses	It is used in private networks.
224.0.0.0/4	Multicast addresses	Reserved for multicast addresses

3.4 ROUTING

We have seen that a router forwards the packet based on the forwarding table. If a datagram is intended for only one node, it is called one-to-one delivery; a unicast routing comes into the scene. If a datagram is intended for more than one destination, it is called many-to-many delivery; a multicast routing comes into the scene. Generally, a source host sends a datagram to its default router in its network. Similarly, a destination host also receives a datagram from the default router in its network. The routers are devices fair forwarding table is required to forward a datagram packet. There are many routes exist which can be used to transmit a datagram.

Datagram Forwarding: Let us understand how forwarding of a packet (datagram) is done. Generally, the IP protocol is used as a connectionless protocol; However, it can be used as a connection-oriented protocol by attaching a level to the datagram and having support from routers. We will discuss, here, connectionless protocol. A datagram is forwarded on the basis of the destination address of the datagram packet by using the forwarding table. Whenever an end system or a router forwards a datagram, it requires a forwarding table. A forwarding table contains the network address with mask, next router's IP address (it is required to get the physical address of next hop), and the interface number. A forwarding table looks like as in **Table 3.5**.

Table 3.5: A forwarding table

network address/mask	next hop IP address	router interface
a.b.c.d/n1	p.q.r.s	I0
e.f.g.h/n2	t.u.v.w	I1
...	...	...
default	x.y.z.m	In

We have seen that a network address is the first address of the block. A destination address only is not sufficient to find which network a packet belongs to. The mask is also stored in a forwarding table. For a given datagram packet, to find which network and to which next hop and interface, an AND operation is performed between the mask and destination address value of the IP datagram. This operation returns an address that is the network address. If this address is matched with the address in the forwarding table, then we choose the given interface and next hop IP address from that row. For the masking, we perform the operation from the longest prefix mask go one by one. If no network address matches with the result from the destination address of the datagram and mask, then it forwards the datagram to the default network address interface.

Internet Structure: Let us look at today's Internet structure to understand the routing of packets in the Internet. Today's Internet is a very complex structure that consists of many backbone structures established and operated by different private companies. There are several service provider networks connected to these big backbone structures. **Figure 3.5** shows an approximate conceptual scenario of the Internet. The backbone networks are connected to each other. Tier -1 or backbone are few, may be 12 or some more. More than 100,000 lower-level ISPs are connected, and private content provider networks, such as Google, are connected. Users are connected to the lower-level ISPs.

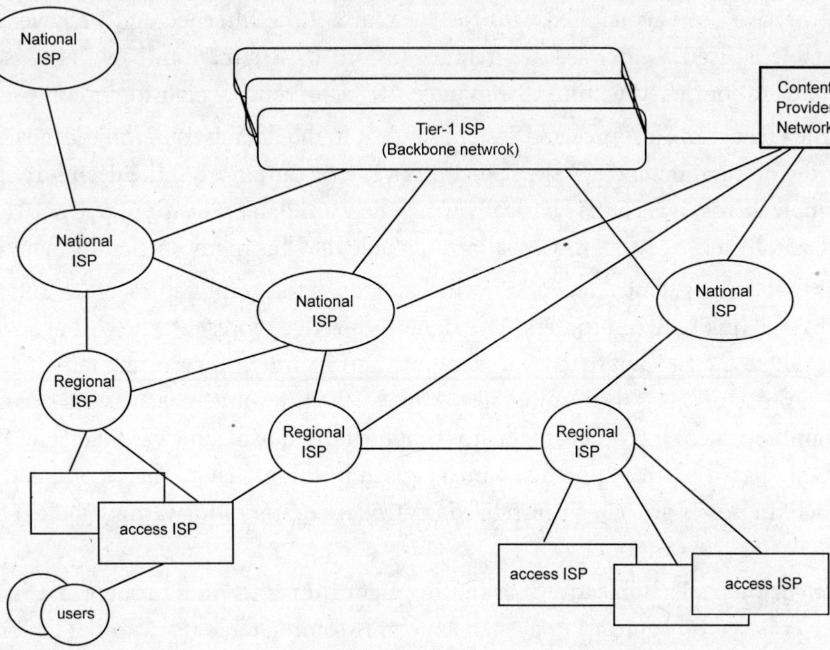

Fig. 3.5: Internet structure

We have seen that the Internet is a very large and complex structure. A forwarding table size at a router will be very big. Searching and updating in that table are very time taking due to huge traffic (i.e., the router maintains its updated information by sending and receiving messages to other routers). To solve this issue, a hierarchy is created. The Internet is divided into many backbones, national ISPs (Internet Service Providers), Regional Internet service providers, and access ISPs. Generally, ISPs have blocks that are large and further divided to make many small, medium, and large networks. ISPs have many routers. Let us say the address of an ISP is a.b.c.d/n. It has many sub-networks into it; however, for outside of this ISP, the rest of the Internet knows only one network address for this ISP (i.e., a.b.c.d/n). Inside the network, ISP has many routers and corresponding forwarding tables to forward packets within the network. The administrator of the ISP has control over its systems. It has many routers as its requirement and executes specific routing algorithms to meet its need. It may also implement its policy on the traffic passing through it. Each ISP is considered as an Autonomous System (AS). A routing protocol is executed at each AS. To deliver a datagram between AS, a global routing protocol is needed. A routing algorithm is executed in each AS, known as intra-AS routing protocol, or interior gateway protocol, or intra-domain routing protocol. The protocol that glues the all the autonomous systems is termed as inter-domain routing protocol, or exterior gateway protocol, or inter-AS routing protocol. We can have different interior gateway protocols, but there is only one exterior gateway protocol that glues all the autonomous systems. Routing Information Protocol (implemented on distance-vector routing algorithm) and Open Shortest Path First (implemented on link-state routing algorithm) are interior gateway protocols. (BGP) Border Gateway Protocol (implemented on path vector routing algorithm, out of scope of this book, see the reference for further study) is exterior gateway protocol. A 16 bits unsigned number is assigned to each autonomous system by ICANN, termed an autonomous number.

Till now, we have been acquainted with the structure of the Internet, and we have also seen how a forwarding table is used to forward a datagram toward its destination. Now let us see how these forwarding tables are computed within AS and inter-AS. Here, routing algorithms come into the scene.

To transmit a datagram, a source end system sends it to the default router in the local networks it is connected. At the destination end system also, it receives a datagram from the default router of its local network. In simple words, it is routers basically which forward datagrams from one network to another network. It is basically a router that has a forwarding table that has many entries for many networks.

A graph is used to represent a network in which a node of the graph represents a router, and an edge represents a physical link between routers. The value at the edge represents the cost of sending a packet between them. There are two approaches to compute and maintain forwarding tables. The first is per router control approach. This is the traditional way in which each router executes the routing algorithm. Each router communicates with other routers to compute the value of a forwarding table. The OSPF and BGP protocols are based on this approach which is used in the Internet. The second is the centralized control approach. In this approach, a centralized controller computes forwarding tables and distributes them.

Routing algorithms: The objective of a routing algorithm is to find a route (that is, a path) from sender to receiver based on some criteria, such as cost. A routing table (forwarding table) is created by the routing algorithm.

We have seen that a network is represented as a graph to formulate a routing problem. There can be two types of algorithms that create forwarding tables. The first type takes global information about the network, i.e., the algorithm knows everything about the whole network (node and associated cost) before creating or computing the forwarding table. This type of algorithm is categorized as a centralized routing algorithm. The distinguishing feature of this algorithm is that it has complete information of the whole network (i.e., connectivity and cost). This algorithm is referred to as Link-State (LS) algorithm because this algorithm is aware of the cost of each link in the network.

In the second type of algorithm, no node (router) has complete information about the whole network. Each node starts with information of the cost of its direct connected link. This algorithm computes the least cost route (path) in a distributed manner by routers iteratively using information exchange among the nodes. This type of algorithm is classified as a decentralized routing algorithm. This algorithm is known as the distance-vector algorithm, reason is that, each node (router) maintains a vector that contains the cost (cost may be a function of the distance between the nodes) to all other nodes.

Let us take an example to understand the path and least cost tree concept. The **Figure 3.6** shows a graph representing a network. A router finds a route (that is, a path) which has least cost to a destination router. For example, in **Figure 3.6,** a path from node P, Q, R, S, T to all other nodes is written in **Table 3.6.**

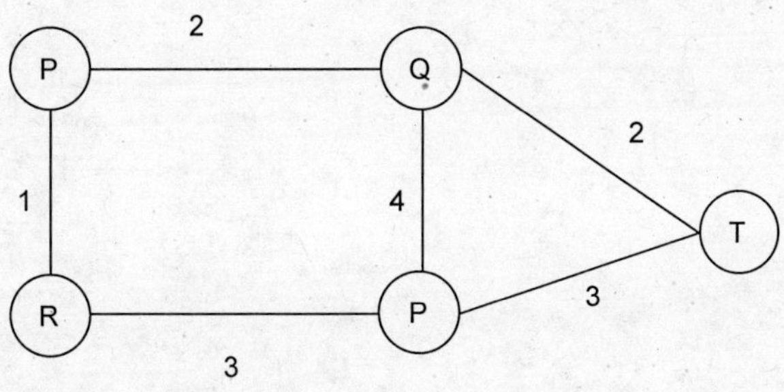

Fig. 3.6: A graph with five nodes representing a network

Table 3.6: Path from Each Node

From Node	Least Cost Path
P	P-Q:2, P-R:1, P-S:4 (P->R->S), P-T:4 (P->Q->T)
Q	Q-P:2, Q-R:3 (Q->P->R), Q-S:4, Q-T:2
R	R-P:1, R-S:3, R-Q:3 (R->P->Q), R-T:5 (R->P->Q->T)
S	S-R:3, S-P:4 (S->R->P), S-Q:4, S-T:3
T	T-Q:2, T-S:3, T-P:4 (T->Q->P), T-R:5 (T->Q->P->R)

Here, we can see that for 5 nodes, there are 20 paths, i.e., if there are n nodes, then n(n -1) paths. If a large number of nodes are present in a network, there would be too many paths. The other way is to represent the same information as the least cost tree. At each node, one least cost tree is created, as shown in **Figure 3.7.** The least cost tree spans the whole graph and records the least cost to all the other nodes from the root node. Therefore, we have only n least cost trees for each node.

3.4.1 Distance-Vector Routing Algorithm

The core of this algorithm is based on the Bellman-Ford equation and the concept of distance-vector. The shortest distance (i.e., least cost) between a source node x and destination node y through intermediary nodes (e.g., a, b, c, ...) is calculated using Bellman-Ford equation. In this, the least cost is given from intermediary nodes to destination note. The equation is

$$LCost_{xy} = \min \{(Cost_{xa} + LCost_{ay}), (Cost_{xb} + LCost_{by}), (Cost_{xc} + LCost_{cy}), \ldots\}$$

$Cost_{xa}$, $Cost_{xb}$, $Cost_{xc}$ are the cost from source node to intermediary nodes, a, b, c. $LCost_{ay}$, $LCost_{by}$, $LCost_{cy}$ are the least cost from the intermediary nodes a, b, c to the destination nodes. $LCost_{xy}$ is the least cost from source x to destination y. Pictorially it is represented in **Figure 3.8.** The purpose of the equation is to calculate new least cost from the previously found least cost.

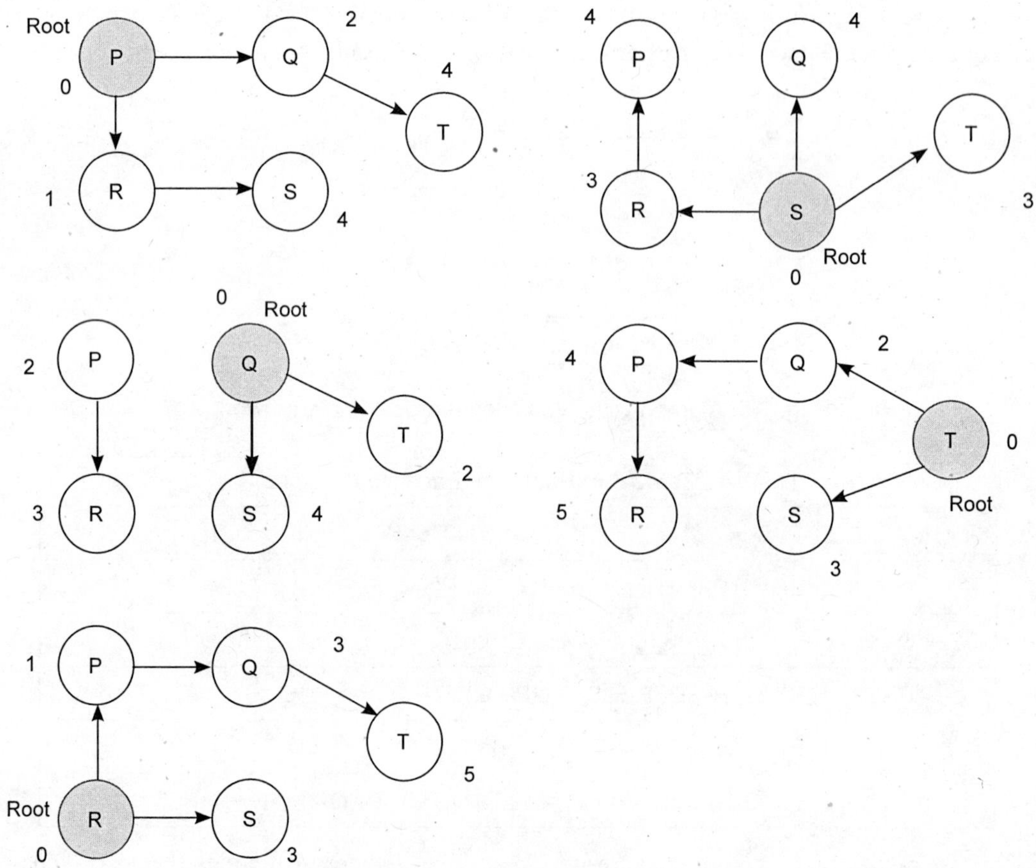

Fig. 3.7: Least cost trees at each node

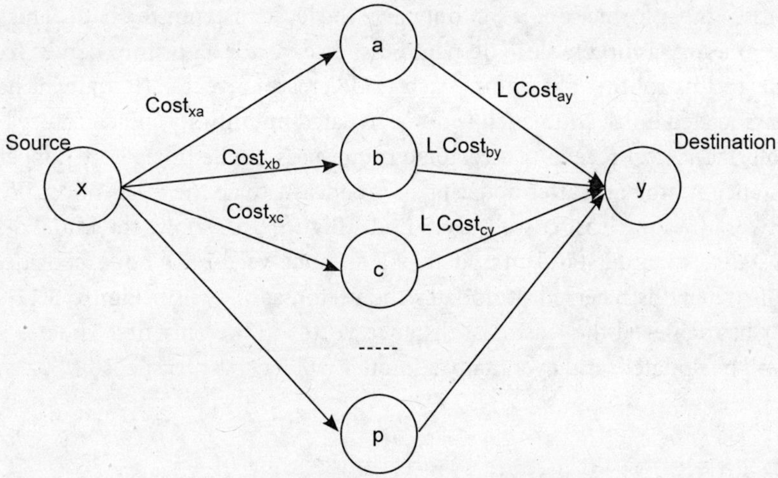

Fig. 3.8: Least cost calculation

We have seen least cost tree. The least cost tree can be represented in the form of a vector storing the distance from the root. For example, the least cost tree in **Figure 3.9** can be represented as one dimensional vector. This one dimensional vector represents the distance from a node to all the other nodes in the graph.

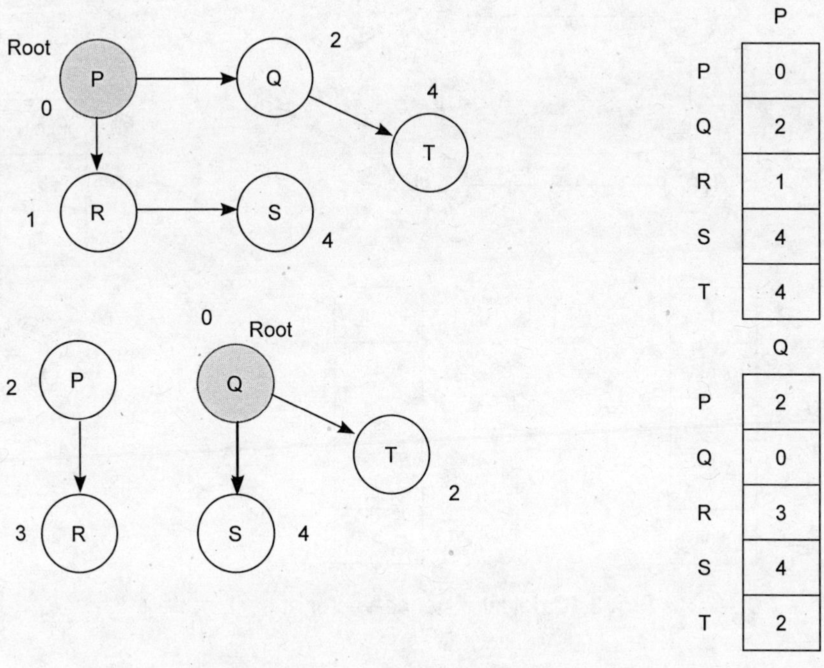

Fig. 3.9: Distance-vector at node P and Q

However, it loses the information; it can only give the least cost, not the path. This distance-vector can be converted to a forwarding table. The name distance-vector algorithm comes from the concept of distance-vector. In this routing algorithm, each node creates a vector (initially, it has only the cost value of directly associated links, and which is not associated put infinity). Each router broadcasts these vectors to each interface. After receiving a vector, a router uses the Bellman-Ford concept to update the distance of its distance-vector, and after updating, it broadcasts to all the other nodes. Eventually, all the routers in the network find the least cost for each node. **Figure 3.10** shows the initial distance-vector at each node. For instance, to understand an update of a distance-vector at a node, consider at node Q, the distance-vector of router P is received. It updates the vector, as shown in **Figure 3.11.** Here, the node Q distance-vector has achieved the least cost distance-vector in the only first update. Similarly, all the distance-vector will be updated, and eventually all nodes will have the least cost.

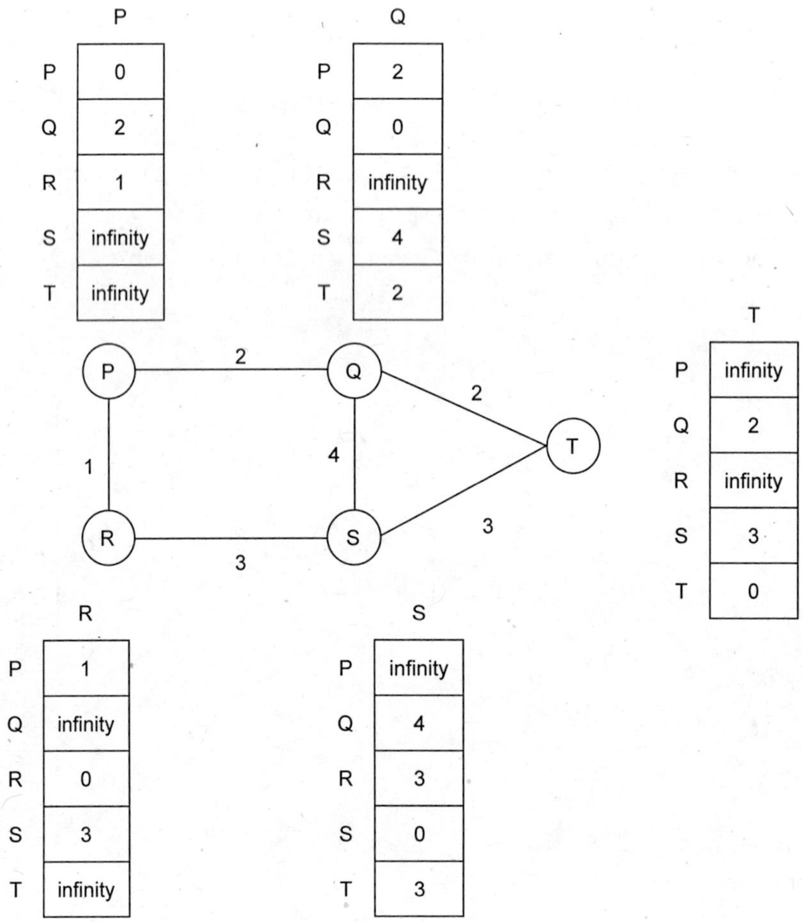

Fig. 3.10: Initial distance-vector at each node

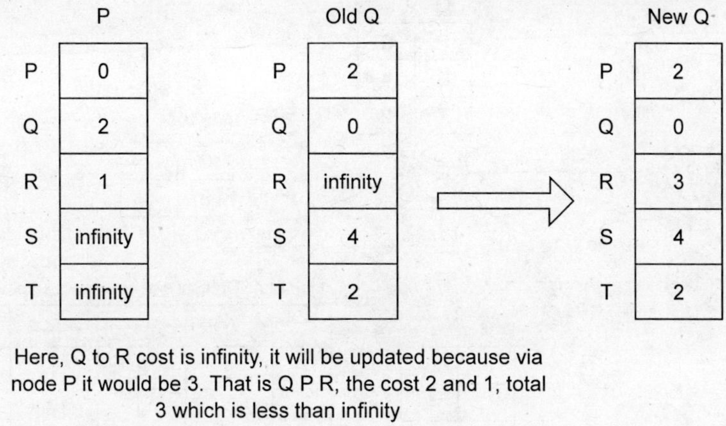

Fig. 3.11: Distance-vector update

Steps of the distance-vector routing:

Step 1. Initialise the distance-vector for all nodes by putting the cost of each directly connected node and putting infinity which is not connected.

Step 2. Repeat forever

Step 2.1. Wait to get any new vector from any neighbour

Step 2.2. Update the cost according to the Bellman-Ford equation

Step 2.3. If there is any change in cost of its distance vector, then sends this updated distance-vector to all the neighbours

Distance-vector routing algorithm suffers from the count to infinity problem. In this algorithm, if a link is broken, that is, the cost is very high (infinity), and this information should be quickly updated to all the routers. But this algorithm takes some time. This problem is termed count to infinity.

Link-State Routing Algorithm

Firstly, the link-state routing algorithm collects the global state information of the whole network. This information is used as input. In practice, global information is obtained by the broadcasting link-state packet (LSP) (which contains the identity and cost of its attached links). Eventually, all the nodes in the network have complete information about the whole network. This collected data is termed a link state database. Secondly, every node runs Dijkstra's algorithm to compute the least-cost path from one node to all other nodes. This algorithm was invented by the computer scientist Edsger W. Dijkstra. An example is explained to understand the working of this algorithm. The example is illustrated in **Figure 3.12.**

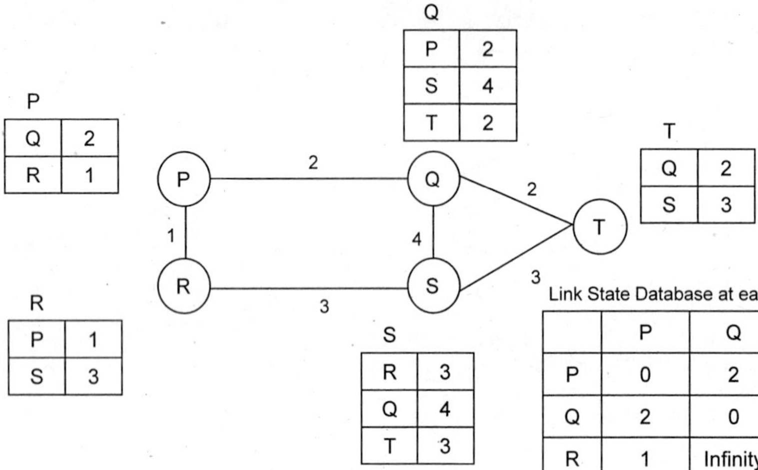

Link State Database at each node (global network information)

	P	Q	R	S	T
P	0	2	1	Infinity	Infinity
Q	2	0	Infinity	4	2
R	1	Infinity	0	3	Infinity
S	Infinity	4	3	0	3
T	Infinity	2	Infinity	3	0

Fig. 3.12: A scenario for global network information

Let us calculate the least cost tree using Dijkstra's algorithm at node P. The calculation is described in **Table 3.7.** At other nodes also, it is computed similarly.

Table 3.7: Least cost tree calculation using Dijkstra's algorithm

		P	Q	R	S	T	Remark, c[u,v] is given in Figure 3.12
	Previous Node	-	-	-	-	-	
Select P as root	Distance from P	0	infinity	infinity	infinity	infinity	Initial values d (cost)
	Previous Node	-	P	P	-	-	
Update cost	Distance from P	0	2	1	infinity	infinity	For **each neighbour v of P**, which is not selected till. If d[P] + c[P,v]<d[v] then d[v] = d[P]+c[P,v], and pre[v] = P here d[P] + c[P,Q]<d[Q] 0+2<infinity, d[Q]=2, previous node = P Similarly d[P]+ c[P,R] < d[R] 0+1<infinity D[R]=1, previous node = P

	Previous Node	-	P	P	-	-	
Select R	Distance from P	0	2	1	infinity	infinity	Because it is least distance and not selected till now
	Previous Node	-	P	P	R	-	
Update cost		0	2	1	4	infinity	For each neighbour of R, which is not selected till now d[R] + c [R,S]<d[S] 1+3<infinity d[S] = 4, previous node = R
Select Q		0	2	1	4	infinity	Because it is least distance and not selected till now
update	Previous Node	-	P	P	R	Q	
Update Cost		0	2	1	4	4	For each neighbour of Q, which is not selected till now d[Q] + c [Q,S]<d[S] 2+4<4 false, so no change d[Q]+c[Q,T] < d[T] 2+2< infinity d[T] = 4, previous node = Q
Select S		0	2	1	4	4	Because it is least distance and not selected till now
Update	Previous Node	-	P	P	R	Q	
Update cost		0	2	1	4	4	For each neighbour of S, which is not selected till now d[S] + c [S,T]<d[T] 4+3<4 false, so no change
Select T		0	2	1	4	4	Because it is least distance and not selected till now
Update	Previous Node	-	P	P	R	Q	
Update Cost		0	2	1	4	4	Here, no node is left for selection, so no change

The least cost can be formed as shown in **Figure 3.13**, from the last entry of previous node and cost in the **Table 3.7**.

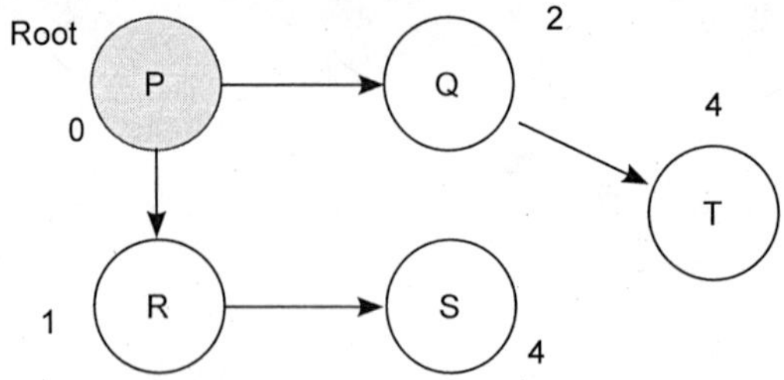

Fig. 3.13: Least cost tree at node P using Dijkstra's algorithm

***Steps of Dijkstra's algorithm*:**

Step 1: The node considers itself a root node. Initialise distance to all nodes to infinity. Initialise distance for root node to zero. Initialize the previous node for all nodes to undefined. For the root node, there is not any previous node.

Step 2: Select a node that has the lowest cost.

Step 3: Modify the cost of the other node if it is not selected till now and is neighbour of the selected node. Modification happens only if the cost is less via the selected node than the previous cost. We also update the previous node if the cost is updated.

Step 4. Repeat Steps 2 and 3 until all nodes are selected.

3.4.3 Routing Information Protocol (RIP) Protocol

RIP protocol is an intra-AS, or intra-domain, or interior routing protocol. Its working is based on the distance-vector routing algorithm. In RIP, integer 16 is used as infinity because it supports maximum hop counts 15. The forwarding table in RIP protocol contains network address, next router address, and hop count. UDP of the transport layer is used to implement RIP. RIP works as a process that uses port number 520. RIP executes in the background in the operating system, termed a daemon process. It means that RIP is a protocol implemented as an application process that is used to create a forwarding table for the network layer. RIP message is made as a UDP packet (by encapsulating UDP header), then it is further made as an IP datagram (by encapsulating IP header). The RIP routers advertise the updates periodically. The time it chooses randomly is between 25 to 35 seconds for periodic advertisements. A RIP message consists of fields, such as request or response command, version number, tag (information about the autonomous system), network address, mask, next hop address, and the number of hops to the destination.

3.4.4 Open Shortest Path First (OSPF) Protocol

It is also an intra-AS, or intradomain, or interior routing protocol. Its implementation uses the link-state routing algorithm. A link cost is based on the round trip time, throughput, etc. A forwarding table is created after getting the tree using Dijkastra's algorithm. The only difference in the forwarding table is the cost value (in RIP, it is simply hop count). RIP is usually used in a small autonomous system. On the other hand, OSPF is used for both small and large autonomous systems. OSPF is also implemented as a program similar to RIP. It also uses an IP datagram to send its message to the other routers. OSPF is a very complex protocol. It also has a provision for authentication.

UNIT SUMMARY

This unit describes the working of the network layer (Internet layer in the TCP/IP protocol stack). The discussion of network performance measurements such as packet loss, throughput, transmission delay, propagation delay, queuing delay, and processing delay. The Internet Protocol (IP), IPv4 address, and IP datagram format are elucidated. The objective of a network layer is to transmit a datagram packet from one host to another host. A network is formed using devices such as routers, switches, and physical links. To deliver a datagram from one host to another host, routers in the network use a routing protocol to make a forwarding table at each router to find a path to travel a datagram packet through the network. The structure of the Internet and routing are discussed. Distance-vector and link-state routing algorithms are discussed in detail. Intra-domain routing protocols, i.e., RIP and OSPF routing protocols, are discussed.

EXERCISES

Multiple Choice Questions (MCQ)

1. Size of IPv4 address is ----- bytes?
   (a) 5 (b) 4 (c) 3 (d) 2
2. Which is not a routing protocol?
   (a) RIP (b) BGP (c) OSPF (d) WWW
3. '\n' in the classless addressing represents?
   (a) suffix (b) intermediate (c) prefix (d) all
4. CIDR stands for?
   (a) Classless Intra-Domain Routing
   (b) Classful Inter-District Routing
   (c) Classless Inter-Domain Routing
   (d) Classful Inter-Domain Routing
5. What is the full form of OSPF?
   (a) Open Shortest Path First
   (b) Open Small Path First
   (c) Open Shortest Path Find
   (d) Open Small Path Find
6. What is the full form of RIP?
   (a) Routing Inter Protocol
   (b) Reserve Intra Protocol
   (c) Reverse Inter Protocol
   (d) Routing Information Protocol
7. Link-state routing algorithm uses?
   (a) Bellman-Ford Equation
   (b) String Match Algorithm
   (c) Dijkstra's Algorithm
   (d) Merge Sort
8. Distance-vector routing uses?
   (a) Quick Sort
   (b) Bellman-Ford Equation
   (c) Kruskal's Algorithm
   (d) Dijkstra's Algorithm

9. Which one is not a private address block?
   (a) 10.0.0.0/8 (b) 172.16.0.0/12
   (c) 192.168.0.0/16 (d) 12.12.13.0/8
10. Which of the following is the limited broadcast address?
   (a) 255.255.255.255/32 (b) 255.255.0.0/16
   (c) 255.0.0.0/8 (d) 255.255.255.0/24

ANSWERS															
1.	(b)	2.	(d)	3.	(c)	4.	(c)	5.	(a)	6.	(d)	7.	(c)	8.	(b)
9.	(d)	10.	(a)												

Questions (Short Answer)

1. Write the tasks performed by the network layer?
2. Describe the forwarding table and its working?
3. Describe classless addressing?
4. What are the rules for dividing a block address into sub-block?
5. What is a mask, and how is it used to find the network address, first address, and last address in a block?
6. What is an autonomous system?
7. Describe the structure of the Internet.
8. What is intra-domain and inter-domain routing?
9. What is a subnetwork?
10. Differentiate between the distance-vector routing algorithm and link-state routing algorithm?
11. Describe (i) throughput, (ii) transmission delay, (iii) propagation delay, (iv) queuing delay, and (v) processing delay.

Questions (Long Answers)

1. Describe Internet protocol version 4. Write about all the fields of the IPv4 header.
2. Explain the Distance-Vector routing algorithm.
3. Describe the Link-State routing algorithm.
4. Write a brief note on OSPF protocol.
5. Write a brief note on RIP Protocol.

PRACTICAL

Aim - 1

Study straight-through and crossover cables and their use from the Internet. Use tools to prepare different wired medium patch cords and test using a cable tester. Also, test and observe for different cable patch cords, which are already prepared by professionals and purchased from the market.

Aim - 2

Explore network configuration settings on computing devices (desktop, laptop, or Mobile). A computer may run the Linux operating system or Windows operating system. Explore IP address setting, subnet mask setting, domain name system setting, gateway setting, and security settings. Also, look Wi-Fi setting and hotspot setting in your mobile phone.

Explore and execute the following command on a computer running the Linux operating system (use 'man' command to see about the command):

1. ifconfig
2. ip
3. traceroute
4. tracepath
5. ping
6. netstat
7. ss
8. dig
9. nslookup
10. route
11. host
12. arp
13. iwconfig
14. hostname
15. curl
16. wget
17. tcpdump

KNOW MORE

Software Defined Network

Software Defined Network (SDN) is a way in which a centralized software program can control the entire network. The control logic from the devices such as router and switch are separated and implemented centrally in a computer. Software defined network contains (i) a controller, which makes possible the centralized management of the network, (ii) a southbound interface, which facilitates communication between a controller and network devices, like routers, switches, and access points, (iii) a northbound interface, this facilitates communication between controller and applications and policy engines. In other words, SDN is an approach that simplifies network operation using centralized software. SDN provides the visibility of the entire network, which helps to implement robust security. A network operator may create a different zone for different levels of security.

REFERENCES AND SUGGESTED READINGS

1. Andrew S. Tanenbaum, Computer Networks, 5th Edition, PHI
2. W. Richard Stevens, TCP/IP Illustrated, Volume-1, Addision Wesley, Second Edition
3. James F. Kurose and Keith W. Ross, Computer Networking: A Top–Down Approach, Pearson, Eight Edition
4. Behrouz A. Forouzan and Firouz Mosharraf, Computer Networks: A Top-Down Approach, Mc Graw Hill Education, Special Indian Edition 2012
5. William Stalling, Computer Networking with Internet Protocols and Technology, Pearson Education, First Edition

Dynamic QR Code for Further Reading

4 Transport and Application Layer

UNIT SPECIFICS

Through this unit, we discuss the following aspects:

- Transport Layer;
- Transmission Control Protocol;
- Application Layer;
- Simple Mail Transfer Protocol;
- Domain Name System;

The unit explains transport layer, protocols of the transport layer - UDP & TCP, application layer, and protocols of the application layer - SMTP and DNS. This unit contains questions for practice. This also provides references for further reading. There is a "Know More" section carefully designed that gives supplementary information based on the context of this unit. A laboratory task is included to get acquainted with the networking devices to make a network.

RATIONALE

This unit on the transport layer and application layer helps students to get an understanding of how a transport layer takes a message from the upper layer, breaks it into segments & implements a reliable and in-order delivery service of packets, and how an application is implemented using application layer protocols. This unit discusses the email application and DNS service. The discussion of protocols, such as SMTP and DNS, helps the students to understand the role of protocol in application development. All these aspects are relevant to understand the working of a network application program.

PRE-REQUISITES

This unit requires unit 1, unit 2, and unit 3 of this book.

UNIT OUTCOMES

The six outcomes of this unit are given below:

U4-O1: Description the transport layer

U4-O2: Description of reliable transmission

U4-O3: Explanation of TCP

U4-O4: Description of application layer

U4-O5: Explanation of SMTP

U4-O6: Explanation of DNS

Unit-4 Outcomes	**EXPECTED MAPPING WITH COURSE OUTCOMES** (1- Weak Correlation; 2- Medium correlation; 3- Strong Correlation)				
	CO-1	**CO-2**	**CO-3**	**CO-4**	**CO-5**
U4-O1	**2**	**3**	**3**	**3**	**3**
U4-O2	2	3	3	2	2
U4-O3	3	3	3	3	3
U4-O4	2	2	3	3	3
U4-O5	3	2	3	3	3
U4-O6	3	2	3	3	3

4.1 TRANSPORT LAYER

A process-to-process communication (also known as logical communication) between the application processes, running on different end systems, is provided by a transport layer. The transport layer protocol is generally implemented on hosts (i.e., end systems), not on switches or routers. At the sender side, an application layer process writes a message (which needs to be sent to the application process) on the socket. Encapsulation at the transport layer converts this message into transport layer packets (commonly known as segments). A segment is created by breaking the message into small chunks, and each chunk is added with a transport layer header to it. The segment is passed to the network layer. A segment is further encapsulated, and a network layer header is added to it to make a network layer packet (commonly known as a datagram). On the receiving machine, the network layer processes the datagram and extracts the segment; further the segment is passed to the transport layer protocol. The transport layer protocol extracts the massages from the segment and identifies the application process (by the port number), and makes it available to that process. The transport layer protocols in the Internet (TCP/IP stack) are (i) TCP (Transmission Control Protocol) and (ii) UDP (User Datagram Protocol).

In the TCP/IP stack, the transport layer is placed between the application and network layer. The task of a transport layer is to provide services to the application layer. The transport layer uses the services of the network layer.

4.1.1 Transport Layer Services

The transport layer protocol facilitates several services to its upper layer. These services are as follows.

Process-to-Process Communication: A host (server or client machine) usually executes (i.e., runs) several processes, as shown in **Figure 4.1.** Each host has an IP address. Network layer protocol transports the datagram from one host to another host (for example, a client machine to a server machine). The datagram may be of process 1, process 2, and so on. The network layer does not care about from which process the datagram belongs. It simply transmits it to the target, that is destination host machine. On the receiving end, the network layer protocol extracts the segment and passes it to the corresponding transport layer protocol, for example, TCP or UDP. The responsibility to pass a message to its corresponding process is handled by transport layer. So, the transport layer establishes a connection between a process executing on an end system to the process executing on another end system, called process-to-process communication.

Identification of a process is done by using a port number. A port number is an integer number (16 bits, ranges zero to 65,535) in TCP/IP protocol stack. A port number used by a client program is known as an ephemeral port number. A process on a server machine also uses a port number, known as a well-known port number.

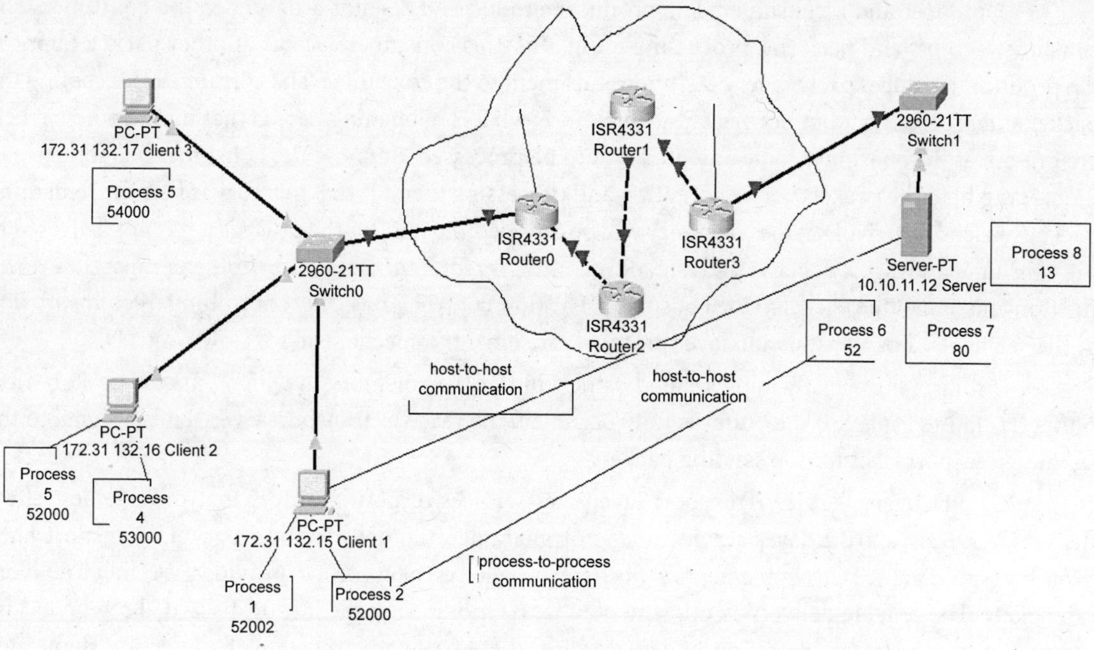

Fig. 4.1: Process-to-process and host-to-host communication

If a client wants to start a communication with a server, it requires the server machine's IP address and the server process port number. A server IP address is obtained by a DNS (Domain Name System) server. The designer made the port number well-known for server processes for all to reduce overhead in obtaining the port number. The port numbers are classified into three categories, namely (i) well-known port numbers, (ii) registered port numbers, and (iii) dynamic port numbers.

Well-known port numbers are from 0 to 1023. It is managed by ICANN. Registered port numbers are from 1024 to 49151. It is not managed by the ICANN. However, it is registered by ICANN to stop collision or duplication by application processes. Dynamic port numbers are from 49152 to 65,535. It is not controlled nor registered. It is used by client processes, also known as temporary or private.

An IP address and a port number collectively form an address referred to as socket address. A socket address identifies a process uniquely on a host. An encapsulation of the message from the upper layer is done by transport layer. At the receiving end, transport layer decapsulates the segment and extracts the message.

Transport layer protocol performs multiplexing and demultiplexing to accomplish process-to-process communication. We can see in **Figure 4.1** that a host can execute multiple processes concurrently; transport layer takes messages from all processes concurrently, referred to as multiplexing. At the receiving end, transport layer protocol demultiplexes the segment to the corresponding process; the destination machine may also execute multiple processes; for example, server machine, as shown in **Figure 4.1,** is running three processes.

Flow Control: The transport layer protocol provides the flow control service. Suppose there is a pair of a producer and a consumer. The producer produces and sends a packet to the consumer. The consumer accepts and performs processing on it; after this consumer accepts another packet. Suppose the producer produces packets very fast and sends them to the consumer. The consumer is accepting the packet and processing it but not very fast. Therefore, what is happening here is that many more packets are present at the consumer to be accepted and to be processed. Suppose the consumer has some small memory to hold the packets before accepting and processing them. If that memory is full, the remaining packets which are arriving at the consumer will be dropped. That is, for the producer, it is not delivered to the consumer and is lost in between. Here, flow control is required; that is, the producer must slow down the transmission of the packet to the consumer. The flow control is basically controlling the transmission of the segments. The transmission layer protocol implements a mechanism for flow control.

Flow control is normally implemented using a buffer (i.e., memory in which packets are stored). A buffer has limited space, if the buffer is fully occupied, the receiver transport layer sends a signal to the sending transport layer to stop sending packets.

Reliable Delivery Service: Transport layer uses services of network layer that provide best-effort delivery service. Network layer service does not guarantee the delivery of a packet. Transport layer protocol (specifically, TCP) implements a mechanism called error control to provide the reliable delivery of packets. The reliable delivery is implemented by (i) monitoring the lost or discarded segments and retransmitting them, (ii) detecting and discarding the corrupted packets, (iii) detecting duplicated packets and discarding duplicate packets, and (iv) rearranging the out-of-order packets.

To detect which packet is lost or which should be retransmitted, or which is arrived out-of-order, each segment is numbered, known as sequence number of the segment. It is an integer number inserted in the transport layer header. At the receiving end, if the packet is lost or corrupted, the transport layer informs (somehow) the sender to retransmit the segment (i.e., packet) using the sequence number of that packet. At the receiving end, if two packets arrive and have the same sequence number, it means it is a duplicate packet. The receiver transport layer discards it. If a packet arrives at receiving end, having a gap in sequence numbers, (for example, packet sequence number 5 arrives, then packet sequence number 3 arrives, and then packet sequence number 1 arrives), it means it is an out-of-order packet. The transport layer protocol simply puts these packets into a buffer and waits for the remaining or informs the sender to retransmit remaining sequence number packets. If the sequence number is of 'm' bits, then the range of sequence number is 0 to 2^m-1. For an instance, if it is 16 bits, the sequence number ranges from 0 to 65535. At the receiving end, the transport layer protocol sends an acknowledgment of receiving a packet from the sender. A sender may use a timer to detect loss of a segment (i.e., packet). At the sender, the transport layer starts the timer when it sends a segment; if the sender does not get any acknowledgment in some specific time, it assumes the packet is lost and resends the packet. We have seen that a buffer is required for the flow control, and sequence number and acknowledgment are required for the error control. A "numbered buffer" is used by the sender's transport layer and receiver's transport layer to meet the requirement of flow control and error control.

Connectionless & connection-oriented service: The application layer passes messages to the transport layer. Segments from these messages are made by transport layer. In connectionless service, the transport layer simply sends to the receiver. The receiver may receive the segment out of order (because the transport layer assumes each segment is independent), and a segment may be lost in the network. In this case, if a segment is lost, the receiver would never know a segment was sent to it. There is no flow control or reliable delivery (i.e., error control) implemented effectively in connectionless service.

A connection is made between the sender's and the receiver's transport layer protocol before the transmission of data, in connection-oriented service. The segments (i.e., packets) transmission only happens after the connection establishment. In the end, when the transmission is finished, the connection is closed.

Congestion Control: Congestion is related to the resources (such as buffers at routers) of the network rather than the end systems. When a network is overflowed by IP datagrams, and packet loss occurs, this situation is referred to as congestion in the network. Although this is pertained to network layer (because IP datagrams are related to network layer), it is handled by transport layer.

4.2 TRANSMISSION CONTROL PROTOCOL (TCP)

TCP is connection-oriented. It is reliable. It implements reliability on top of unreliable Internet Protocol (IP). The TCP header structure is shown in **Figure 4.2.** The TCP header size is twenty bytes to sixty bytes. It contains the port numbers of the communicating processes for distinguishing the processes running on a host, i.e., process-to-process transmission of data. The reliability is implemented using the numbering of each byte of the data (i.e., each byte has a sequence number), acknowledgment, retransmission, and error control. Therefore, the header of TCP contains the sequence number field, acknowledgment field, control bits, and checksum field. To make a connection, the flag bits, such as RST (it means reset the connection), SYN (it means synchronize sequence number), and FIN (it means close the connection) are contained in the TCP header. There is a filed urgent pointer; it is indicting the sequence number of the last byte in the data that are part of urgent data. URG – urgent pointer bit is a flag that indicates the data has some urgent data also. The header length is varied from 20 bytes to 60 bytes; therefore, a header length field is also part of the TCP header. TCP implements flow control. Hence, the window size field is contained in the TCP header.

<table>
<tr><td colspan="2">port number of source process
(16 bits)</td><td colspan="2">port number of destination process
(16 bits)</td></tr>
<tr><td colspan="4">sequence number
(32 bits)</td></tr>
<tr><td colspan="4">acknowledgment number
(32 bits)</td></tr>
<tr><td>Header
4 bits</td><td>Reserved
6 bits</td><td>Control Bits
6 bits</td><td>Window size
16 bits</td></tr>
<tr><td colspan="3">Checksum (16 bits)</td><td>urgent pointer (16 bits)</td></tr>
<tr><td colspan="4">Options (40 bytes)</td></tr>
<tr><td colspan="4">Data</td></tr>
</table>

Fig. 4.2: TCP header structure and data

Port number of source process: The port number of the source application process is contained in this 16 bits field.

Port number of destination process: The port number of the destination application process is contained in this 16 bits field.

Sequence number: Each byte of a message is numbered for reliable transmission. This number is called a sequence number. A 32 bits field is to store the first byte's sequence number of data in the segment.

Acknowledgment number: This field is also 32 bits. It contains the sequence number of next segment expected by receiver. It is used to implement reliable transmission.

Header Length: It is a 4 bits field to store the length of the TCP header length. We can get the header length value by multiplying 4 into the value of this field. For example, if the value is 1111 = 15, the header length is 15*4=60 bytes.

Reserved Bits: This is reserved. Two bits of it are used for CWR flag and ECE flag. Both flags are used for explicit congestion notification.

Control Bits: This field has 6 control bits, namely, URG, ACK, PSH, RST, SYN, and FIN. If URG flag is set, it means urgent pointer field is a valid. If ACK flag is set, it means the acknowledgment field is valid. PSH flag indicates that data in the segment should be passed to the upper layer application process immediately. RST flag indicates for resetting the connection. SYN flag indicates for synchronizing sequence number. FIN flag indicates termination of TCP connection.

Window Size: The window size is contained in this 16 bits field. This is used in flow control.

Checksum: This is a 16 bits field for the detection of any error in the segment. There are many techniques for error detection, for example, parity bit, cyclic redundancy check.

Urgent Pointer: This 16 bits field holds the value which is added into the sequence number field value to calculate the last byte's sequence number of urgent data.

Options: This field stores optional information of TCP, which may be used for special purposes, for example, maximum segment size, selective acknowledgment, timestamps, and widow scaling.

4.2.1 TCP Connection, Data Transmission, and Termination

Let us understand how a TCP connection is made for a segment transmission. An application process passes message (i.e., data) to the TCP. The TCP encapsulates the data into segments. A segment is further encapsulated into an IP datagram (by network layer). An IP datagram is further encapsulated into a data link layer frame. The TCP assigns an integer number to each byte of the data for reliable delivery to the destination process. The first byte of the message is numbered with any arbitrary number from 0 and 2^{32} - 1. The number 0 is not necessary to assign to the first byte; it can be any arbitrary number between 0 to 65535. For example, if an application process passes data of 8000 bytes to the TCP, the TCP numbers the first byte, say, 2051, and the last byte is numbered 10,050. The data is broken into many segments (which are encapsulated with a TCP header). Each segment has a number called a sequence number. Generally, a sequence number of a segment is the number of the first byte of the data of the segment. For example, if each segment carries 1000 bytes, the first segment will carry data byte number from 2051 to 3050, the second segment will carry data from 3051 to 4050, and so on. Therefore, first segment's sequence number is 2051, second segment's sequence number is 3051, and so on. The first segment's sequence number is known as Initial Sequence Number (ISN).

TCP provides full-duplex communication; each sender and receiver can send/receive segments simultaneously in both directions. Each TCP at each end system maintains its own sending buffer and receiving buffer. Each segment also contains an acknowledgment number. The objective of an acknowledgment number is to confirm the sender that what segment and data bytes the receiver TCP received. This acknowledgment number is the value that indicates the next segment the receiver TCP is expecting to receive. It is also cumulative, which means the acknowledgment number indicates that till that point, all the data bytes are received. For an instance, if an acknowledgment number is 3051, it indicates that the receiver has received data till 3050 data bytes numbers and is expecting the segment with the number 3051.

Note: An application process sends data bytes to its TCP. TCP puts these data bytes into its sending buffer. After connection establishment, the TCP takes these bytes from sending buffer and makes a segment and sends. The question is how many maximum bytes can be put into a segment. In other words, how a Maximum Segment Size (MSS) (i.e., the data bytes only, not including the TCP header, a confusing terminology) is determined or decided. It is typically 1460 bytes. The Ethernet and the PPP link layer protocol send 1500 bytes, i.e., the maximum transfer unit. The MSS is determined by finding out the largest size of the frame that can be sent by link layer protocol. Generally, we take care after adding the TCP/IP header and data bytes; it should not be greater than the maximum transfer unit of the link layer. Another question is when TCP takes data from its sending buffer and sends it. The answer is that it takes and sends on its own convenience [RFC 793].

A window is simply defining the boundary from the start data byte and end data byte which is currently considered for the transmission/processing. This window slides, i.e., go ahead if current data bytes are sent/processed successfully. This window size may shrink (in case of congestion) or may enlarge decided by TCP. So, the TCP uses the sliding window. **Figure 4.3** shows buffer, window, segment, datagram, and frame.

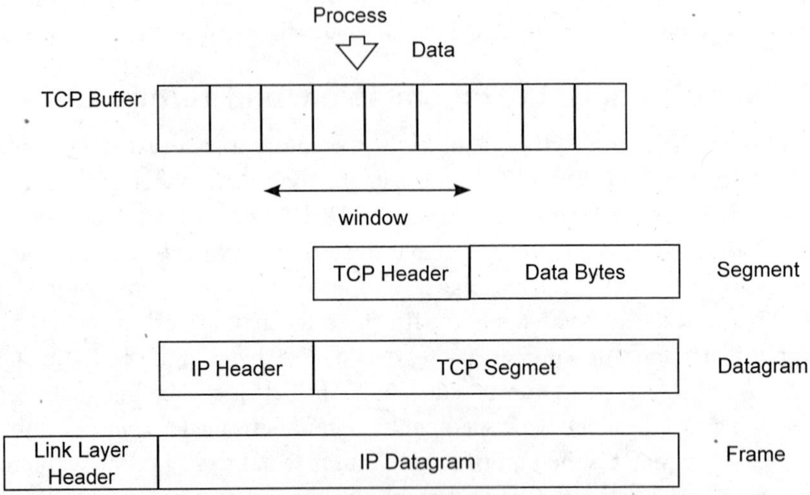

Fig. 4.3: Buffer, window, segment, datagram, frame

TCP makes a connection before transmitting segments of data. This connection is between the sender TCP and receiver TCP running at hosts. This TCP connection seems a logical path between sender TCP and receiver TCP; however underlying network layer is connectionless, that is, each IP datagram is sent/received independently.

Connection establishment: TCP supports full-duplex transmission of data, i.e., sender and receiver TCP both send and receive data segments simultaneously. An abstract view is presented in **Figure 4.4.**

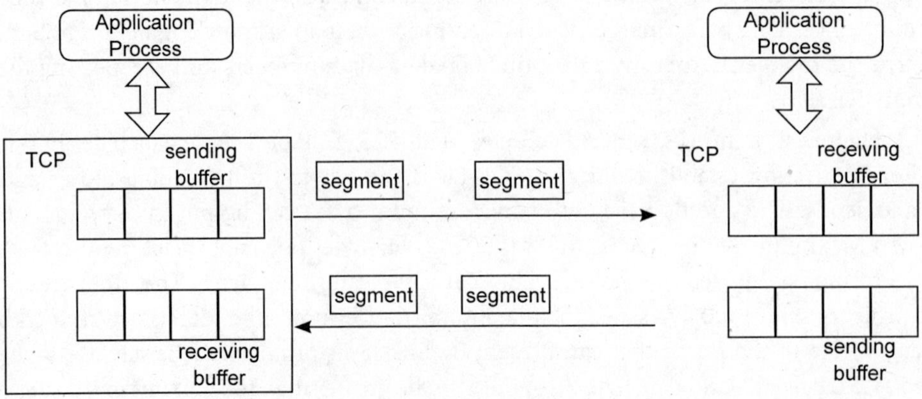

Fig. 4.4: Abstract view of full-duplex connection

The connection establishment means that TCP (TCP at both client and server machine or both communicating TCP) initializes the communication by taking approval from the other. That is, both TCP agree that they are going to send/receive data. A connection is established using **three-way handshaking**. To understand a connection establishment, let us take an example. A client chat application process wants to send chat text data, let 3000 bytes, using TCP. The server chat application process initializes its TCP to become ready to accept a connection (i.e., passive open) from any process. The client chat application process initiates a request to its TCP for an active open; that is, it tells its TCP to make a connection to the chat application process server. Now TCP starts the three-way handshake for establishing a connection.

Step 1: The client chat application process's TCP sends a segment, termed 'SYN' segment. As We have already seen, a segment structure in **Figure 4.2,** it has many fields, including SYN. In this segment, the SYN flag is set (i.e., the value of this bit is 1). The purpose of the SYN segment is to synchronize sequence number. That means the server TCP gets informed that the client TCP will send segments that will have the sequence number onward. This SYN segment has the first sequence number (a random number between 0 to 65535), referred to as initial sequence number. This SYN segment does not have any acknowledgment number or window size. This segment consumes one sequence number because this segment has to be acknowledged by the receiver TCP but does not carry any data. The consumption of a sequence number simply means that it is used to number a data byte, but here, in this case, no data byte is sent in the SYN segment.

Step 2: The server TCP transmits a segment as a reply having two flags SYN and ACK are set. This segment has two purposes. It acts as a SYN segment for making connection in the reverse direction (that is, from server to client). The sequence number in this packet tells the client TCP that the server TCP is using this sequence number onwards to number its data bytes. The second purpose is that it acknowledges the first SYN segment from the client. It also has a receiver window size which will be used by the client TCP for flow control. This segment also does not carry data bytes, however consumes one sequence number.

Step 3: Now client TCP sends the third segment to acknowledge the arrival of the second segment. It has an ACK flag set and an acknowledgment number. Note, some implementation allows to send the first chunk of data in the third segment of this connection establishment phase. **Figure 4.5** shows the connection establishment pictorially.

Data transmission: Data can be transferred in both directions. In this example, a chat client process sends 3000 data bytes. Let each segment carry 1000 data bytes. In three segments, all data will be sent by the client, as shown in **Figure 4.5**. At the server TCP, data bytes are received and stored in the buffer. These data are delivered to the server application process when the server application process is ready. There is a PSH flag in the segment. If it is set, the server TCP passes the data (message) to the application process as fast as possible. There is a URG flag; it indicates urgent data.

Connection termination: A TCP connection can be closed in two ways (i) three-way handshaking (ii) four-way handshaking.

Step 1: To close the connection, the client application process initiates a close request to its client TCP. The client TCP creates a segment, termed as FIN segment. The FIN flag is set in this segment. It may also contain the last chunk of data, or it may be only a control segment.

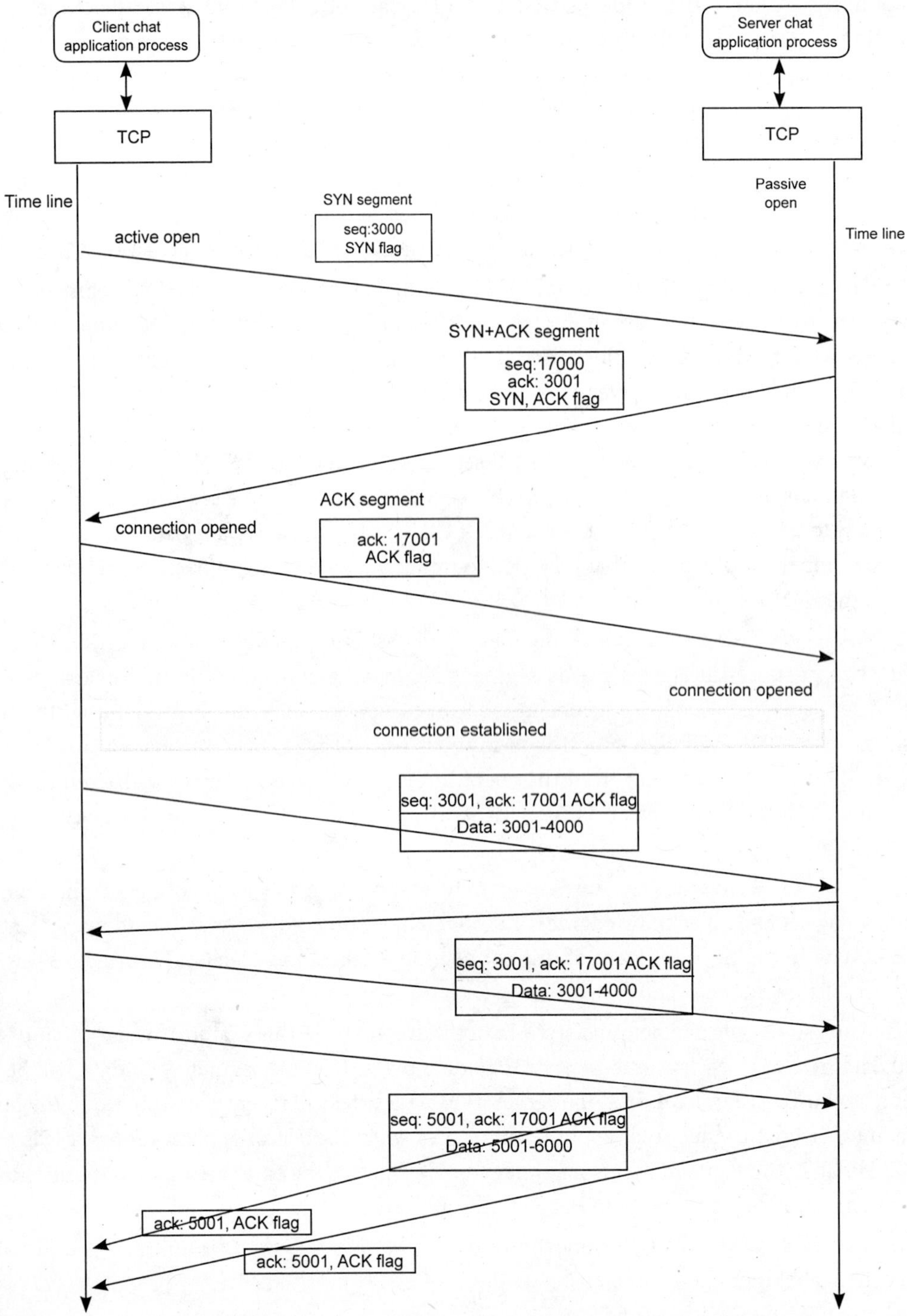

Fig. 4.5: Connection establishment and data transmission

Step 2: The FIN segment is received by the server TCP. After receiving, server TCP informs the server application process. Now, the server TCP transmits the second segment, termed FIN+ACK segment; that is, FIN and ACK flags are set. This segment has two purposes (i) to indicate the acceptance of the FIN segment and (ii) to declare the termination of the connection of the other direction.

Step 3: The client TCP transmits the ACK segment to confirm the acceptance of the second segment (ACK+SYN segment). **Figure 4.6** shows the three-way handshaking termination.

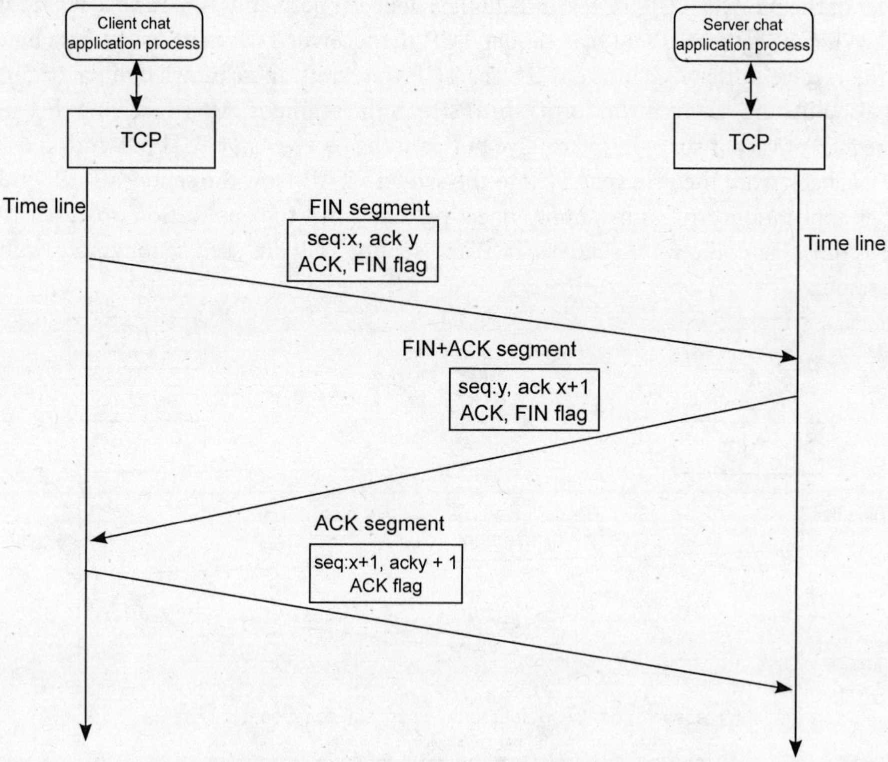

Fig. 4.6: Three-way handshake connection termination

In the **four-way handshaking**, a connection can be half closed, that is, the connection from the client to the server can be closed; but, it is possible to remain open the connection between the server to client path and vice versa. **Figure 4.7** shows the four-way handshaking termination.

4.2.2 Flow Control

TCP uses two windows for transmitting data, namely, send window and receive window. For the full-duplex, it has four windows, two for each direction.

A sender TCP sends segments to the receiver TCP. Receiver TCP gets this segment and extracts the data bytes and puts them into the receive buffer. The application process, which is associated with this TCP, reads data from this receive buffer. The application may not read (consume) data bytes from the receive buffer immediately; it may be busy doing some other tasks. Here, data bytes are resided in the receiver TCP's receive buffer. If the sender application through the sender TCP sends many other segments, the receive buffer will be overflown. To stop this overflowing, the flow control comes into the scene. Flow control simply tries to match the speed of the sender to the consumption (reading) at the receiver. If data bytes are residing in the receiver's TCP receive buffer, the vacant space in the receiver's TCP receive buffer will be less. Hence, this vacant space of the buffer varies according to the receiver application process consumption (reading). The sender TCP maintains a variable known as 'receive window'. By maintaining this variable, the sender TCP has an idea of the vacant space in the receive buffer of the receiver TCP. TCP is full-duplex; hence at both ends, the receive window variable is maintained. When a segment is sent by a sender TCP, the receiver TCP extracts the data bytes and puts them into the receive buffer. When the receiver's TCP transmits an acknowledgment segment or data segment, it also puts the received window (**rwnd**) size in the segment. After receiving this segment, the TCP gets the idea of vacant space in the receive buffer at the receiver's TCP. The (rwnd) receive window size acts as feedback from the receiver's TCP to the sender's TCP. Now the sender's TCP sends feedback to the sender application process by simply rejecting data from the application process (in case if the send buffer is full). Here, the word sender's TCP and sender TCP are used synonymously, the meaning of both are same.

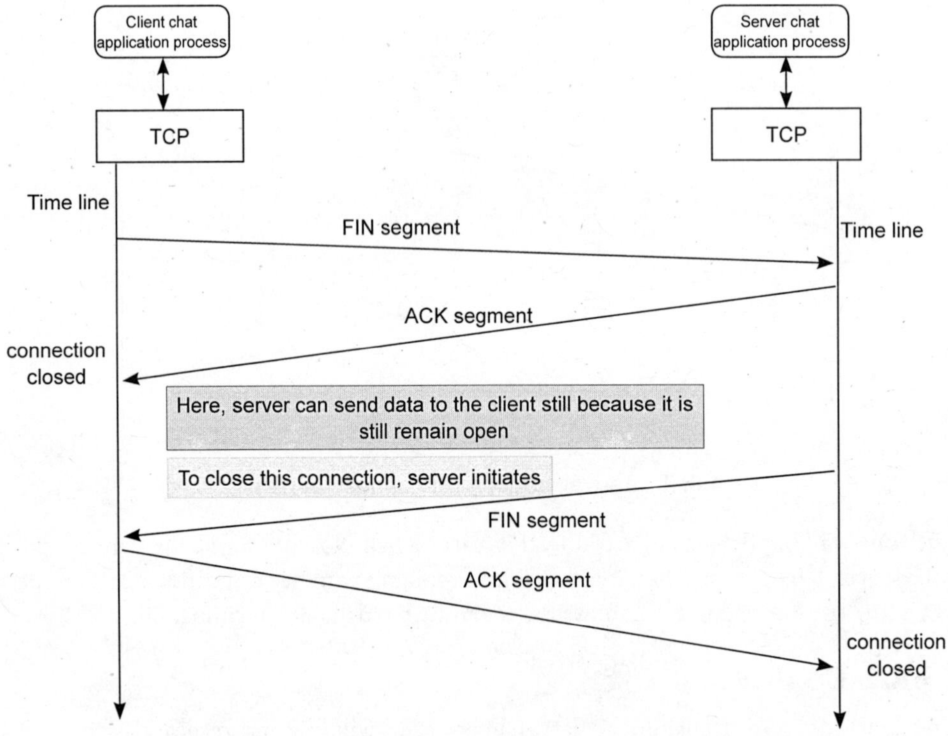

Fig. 4.7: Connection termination, half closed, four-way handshaking

4.2.3 Error Control

TCP provides reliable data delivery. It means that the application process receives data without error, in order, without duplication, or any loss. The reliability is achieved through the mechanism called error control. The Error control is implemented using a sequence number, acknowledgment, time-out, retransmission, and checksum. The task performed by the error control is (i) detecting corrupted segments (using checksum) and dropping them, (ii) storing segments, which are out-of-order, until the missing segments arrive (using buffer and sequence number), (iii) resending the last segment (using acknowledgment and time-out and retransmission), and (iv) detecting duplicate segments and dropping it (using sequence number).

We have already seen that each data byte is numbered to keep track of every byte. A sequence number of a segment is, generally, the assigned number of the first data byte of the segment. An acknowledgment is a number that indicates to the sender that what is the next sequence number is expected by the receiver and indicates till that number all the data bytes are received. For an instance, if an acknowledgment number is 9001, the meaning is that the receiver TCP expects the next segment having segment number 9001, and till number 9000, each data byte is received successfully. Checksum is the number that is used to detect error (single bit error or burst error) in the segments. The techniques which are used to detect errors are, namely, parity check, check summing method, and cyclic redundancy check.

Round-Trip Time: The RTT is defined as the time taken by a segment to reach the destination and the acknowledgment from the destination to the sender. Generally, the sender TCP maintains a timer for each connection, called retransmission time-out. When a sender's TCP transmits a segment, it starts the timer. If the sender's TCP does not get an acknowledgment for that segment (it assumes the segment is lost in the network) and the timer expires, it retransmits this segment. The timer value, that is, the retransmission time-out value, is decided on the basis of round-trip time. A sender TCP also retransmits a segment after getting three duplicate acknowledgments (i.e., without waiting for retransmission time-out). Three duplicates mean one original plus three other same. This retransmission is termed **fast retransmission**. To ensure the in-order delivery of data bytes, TCP stores the out-of-order received segments in the receive buffer and passes them to the application process only when the missing segments are received. The idea of reliable delivery can be studied through the concepts of the Selective Repeat and Go-back-N protocol. In practice, TCP is a mixture of both.

4.2.4 Congestion Control

The buffer (receive buffer at the TCP) will not be overflowed by the sender TCP is ensured by the flow control. However, congestion may happen in the network, e.g., the buffers of routers may be full. A router gets datagrams from multiple senders, there is always a chance that the router buffer can be full. Routers and datagrams are dealt by IP (Internet Protocol). But, IP does not deal the congestion of the network. The network's congestion is also dealt by the TCP. However, IP and TCP may implement network-assisted congestion control optionally. In a network-assisted technique, a router explicitly sends feedback to the sender about the congestion. Here, we will see the traditional approach.

Like receive window (rwnd) variable, TCP maintains a congestion window (cwnd) variable to control and monitor a congestion in the network. Therefore, the sender has to decide the window size for creating segments based on the (rwnd) receive window and (cwnd) congestion window. Therefore, the window size is calculated as minimum of cwnd and rwnd.

In the management of a congestion, firstly, a sender detects a congestion in the network. The sender TCP determines that there is congestion if a time-out happens or three duplicate acknowledgments receives. If an acknowledgment is not received within the time-out period, the sender TCP assumes the segment is lost due to congestion. If three duplicate acknowledgments are received, it is also considered due to congestion but less congestion than as time-out.

TCP congestion control algorithm has three states, namely (i) slow start, (ii) congestion avoidance, and (iii) fast recovery.

Slow start: This is the start state of the congestion algorithm. The algorithm starts with initializing the congestion window (cwnd) value to 1 MSS. MSS means maximum segment size. The algorithm increases cwnd by 1 MSS every time when it receives an acknowledgment. For example, the cwnd is calculated in **Table 4.1,** assuming that the sender is receiving acknowledgment for each segment separately.

Table 4.1: Calculation of congestion window size in slow start state

cwnd = 1MSS	
cwnd = cwnd +1 = 1 +1 = 2 MSS	Send segment s1 Receive ack1
cwnd = cwnd +1 = 2+1 = 3 cwnd = cwnd +1 = 3+1 =4	Send segment s2 Send segment s3 Receive ack2 Receive ack3
cwnd = cwnd + 1 = 4+1 =5 cwnd = cwnd + 1 = 5+1 =6 cwnd = cwnd + 1 = 6+1 =7 cwnd = cwnd + 1 = 7+1 =8	Send segment s4 Send segment s5 Send segment s6 Send segment s7 Receive ack4 Receive ack5 Receive ack6 Receive ack7

The growth of sending segments is increasing exponentially. Here three cases arise (i) no loss of segment, (ii) time-out occurs (i.e., loss of a segment), (iii) three duplicate acknowledgments (that is less severe congestion). There is a variable named 'ssthreshold' for slow start threshold is maintained to limit the exponential growth. When the cwnd value crosses this ssthreshold value, congestion algorithm switches to the congestion avoidance state.

Case 1 (***no loss of segment***): If the algorithm is in the slow start state, it increases the cwnd value exponentially, at every RTT (as shown in Table 4.1) and transmits segments. After that, it compares the cwnd value to the slow start threshold value. If cwnd value is less, it remains in the same state (i.e., slow start); otherwise it switches to the congestion avoidance state.

Case 2 (***time-out occurs for a segment***): Irrespective of the state, the algorithm switches to slow start state and modifies the value of ssthreshold to cwnd/2 (i.e., ssthreshold value is also dynamically learned), sets cwnd = 1 MSS. After this, retransmit the lost segment.

Case 3 (three duplicate acknowledgments received): If three duplicate acknowledgments are received, the algorithm switches to fast recovery state by setting ssthreshold = cwnd/2 and cwnd = ssthreshold + 3 MSS. After this, it retransmits the lost segment.

Congestion Avoidance: In the congestion avoidance mode, the value of cwnd does not increase exponentially (i.e., doubling the value every RTT) but increases by one MSS every RTT (round-trip time).

In other words, cwnd value increases by (MSS/cwnd)xMSS on receiving each acknowledgment. For an instance, let the MSS size is 1460 bytes, and the cwnd is 8 MSS = 8 x 1460 =11,680 bytes. Suppose it sends 8 segments; for each segment, it receives an acknowledgment. After receiving each acknowledgment, the cwnd will be updated as shown in **Table 4.2.**

Table 4.2: Calculation of congestion window size in congestion avoidance state

cwnd = 8MSS	
	Send seg1
	Send seg2
	Send seg3
	Send seg4
	Send seg5
	Send seg6
	Send seg7
	Send seg8
cwnd=cwnd+(1460/11680)x1460=8MSS + (1/8)MSS	Received ack1
cwnd=8MSS + (1/8)MSS + (1/8)MSS	Received ack2
cwnd=8MSS + (1/8)MSS + (1/8)MSS + (1/8)MSS	Received ack3
cwnd=8MSS + (1/8)MSS + (1/8)MSS + (1/8)MSS + (1/8)MSS	Received ack4
cwnd=8MSS + (1/8)MSS + (1/8)MSS + (1/8)MSS + (1/8)MSS + (1/8)MSS	Received ack5
cwnd=8MSS + (1/8)MSS + (1/8)MSS + (1/8)MSS + (1/8)MSS + (1/8)MSS + (1/8)MSS	Received ack6
cwnd=8MSS + (1/8)MSS + (1/8)MSS + (1/8)MSS + (1/8)MSS + (1/8)MSS + (1/8)MSS + (1/8)MSS	Received ack7
cwnd=8MSS+(1/8)MSS+(1/8)MSS+(1/8)MSS+(1/8)MSS+(1/8)MSS+(1/8)MSS+(1/8)MSS+(1/8)MSS = 8MSS+(8/8)MSS= 9 MSS	Received ack8

The cwnd is updated as cwnd = cwnd + (MSS/cwnd)MSS on receiving each acknowledgment. In this state also when a time-out occurs for a segment, it switches to the slow start state by setting ssthreshold = cwnd/2, and cwnd = 1 MSS. If three duplicate acknowledgment occurs, it goes to fast recovery state by setting ssthreshold = cwnd/2 and cwnd = ssthreshold + 3 MSS. It simply means that it does not decrease congestion window size (cwnd) to 1 MSS when switches from congestion avoidance mode to fast recovery mode.

Fast Recovery: In this state, if a new acknowledgment is received for a segment, it switches to congestion avoidance state by setting cwnd = sstreshold. If a time-out occurs in this state for a segment, it switches to the slow start state by setting ssthreshold = cwnd/2 and then cwnd =1MSS. The algorithm remains in the same state (i.e., in the fast recovery state) if it receives a duplicate acknowledgment, it also increases cwnd value by one MSS, i.e., the cwnd = cwnd + 1 MSS. **Figure 4. 8** shows how the congestion algorithm moves from one state to another state. The TCP congestion algorithm is termed AIMD (Additive Increase Multiplicative Decrease Algorithm).

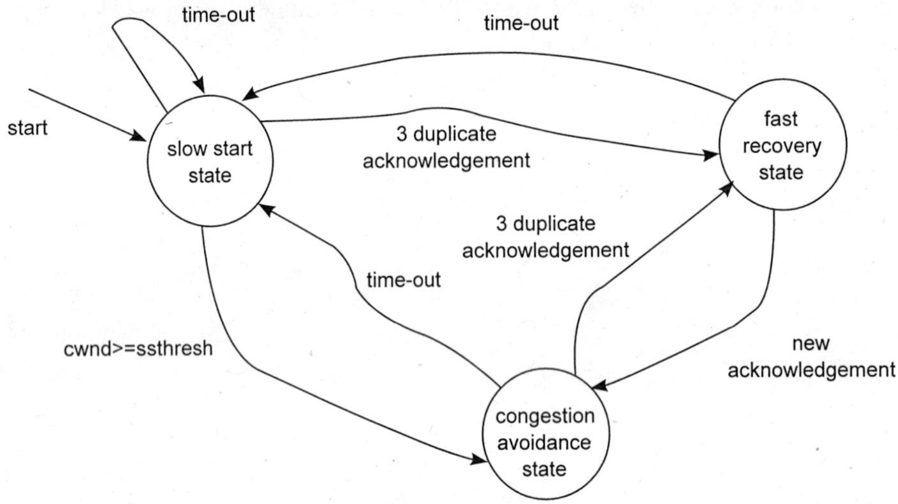

Fig. 4.8: Congestion control states

4.3 APPLICATION LAYER

The objective of network infrastructure (e.g., the Internet) is to transmit messages (data) from one machine (end system/host) to another machine (end system/host). The end system is a desktop, laptop, smartphone, server machine, etc. The question is who requires transmitting data from one end system to another end system. The entity which requires to transmit data is a program which is commonly known as an application program or network application program. The network application program executes on an end system and transmits data to a program that is executing on different end system. The end systems are connected through the network infrastructure (i.e., through devices and protocols). The example of network application programs are email, remote access to computers, file transfers, web surfing, searching, e-commerce, video conferencing (e.g., Skype, Google hangout, Facetime, Zoom, Microsoft Teams), social network applications (e.g., Twitter, Instagram, Facebook), movies and drama on demand (e.g., Netflix, YouTube), mobile payment applications (e.g., Paytm, PhonePe, BHIM, GooglePay), location-based road traffic forecasting applications, and messaging applications (e.g., WhatsApp, Telegram). These network application programs are written using the languages such as C, Java, Python, PHP, Nodejs, etc.

A network application program is written in a certain way, known as application architecture, this is simply how an application program is structured, which is going to run and communicate on the multiple end systems. There are two architectures (i) peer-to-peer and (ii) client-server. The client-server architecture is shown in **Figure 4.9;** a server program always runs and responds to a client program request. Browsers or mobile applications are examples of client programs that execute on the end system, such as a desktop, laptop, or mobile phone. The server has a fixed IP address and always runs. A client program can communicate with the server by sending packet the server machine by using fixed IP address. In peer-to-peer architecture, a client communicates directly with another client. There is no need for a dedicated server. Peer-to-peer network application is BitTorrent file-sharing application.

Note: The limitation of a single server is that it cannot serve all the requests from all over the world. To serve all the requests for an application (e.g., search engines, such as Google, Bing, Baidu; emails, such as Gmail and Yahoo; e-commerce, such as Amazon, Alibaba; social network platforms, such as Twitter, Instagram, Facebook), a data center is built. Applications are running on data centers that contain a very large number of server machines.

Fig. 4.9: Client server architecture

We have learned that a network application executes on a client machine and a server machine. The application needs to communicate through the network infrastructure. In the terminology of an operating system, a program that is running is known as a process. The operating system provides a socket interface. If a process running on an end system wants to transmit data to a process executing on different end system connected through the network infrastructure, it simply puts its data on the socket, which is provided by the operating system on its own end system, as shown in **Figure 4.10**. On the other end, the receiving end system reads the data from its own socket. The data from one socket to the other socket passes through the protocol stack and several devices and links of the network. The application developer does not worry about how data is transmitted. The developer simply uses the transportation service of the network infrastructure.

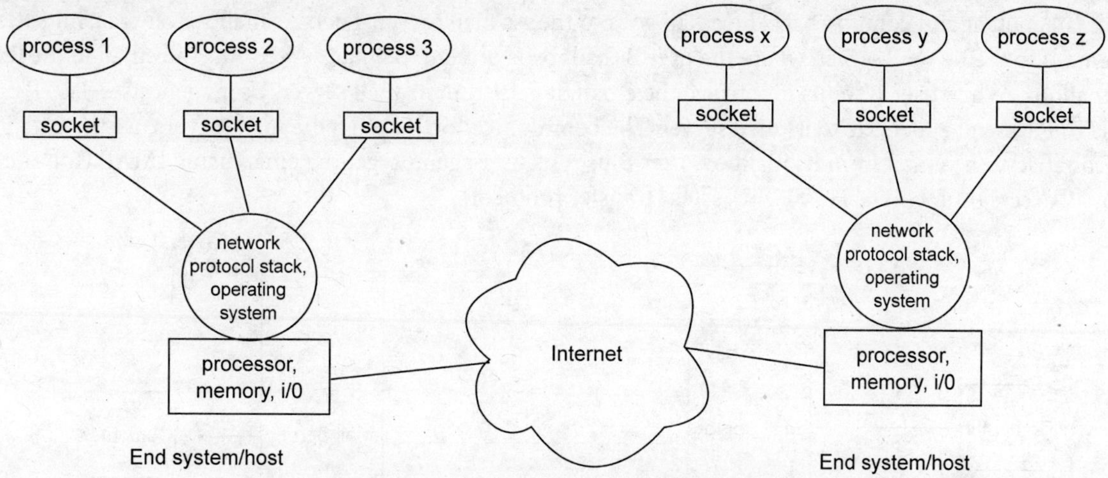

Fig. 4.10: Process-to-process communication

On the end system, there may be multiple processes running. To distinguish a process, an integer number is associated with it, known as port number. The pair of port number and IP address is sufficient to distinguish any process on the Internet.

A socket file acts as an interface between the network application process and transport layer. The network application process gets the services, such as reliable data transfer, connection-oriented service (TCP), and connectionless service (UDP) through the socket.

Note - User Datagram Protocol: UDP is a transport layer protocol, connectionless, unreliable and provides process-to-process communication. The beauty of user datagram protocol is that it has very less overhead. If an application needs to transmit small messages and reliability is not a concern, UDP is used. UDP packet is referred to as user datagram. It does not implement flow control, error control (except checksum), and congestion control. UDP is used in trivial file transfer protocol, simple network management protocol, routing information protocol, real-time applications, etc.

What is an application layer protocol? What are the purposes of this protocol? A network application process communicates to the other process by sending data, i.e., messages. A message has a structure that is known by the communicating processes, so they can understand the meaning of it. Here, application layer protocol comes into the scene. Application layer protocol defines (i) structure of a message, (ii) type of messages (i.e., request or response), (iii) semantic of the fields in the message, and (iv) rules for sending and responding of message.

The application layer protocols are SNMP (Simple Network Management Protocol), HTTP (HyperText Transfer Protocol), NFS (Network File System), SMTP (Simple Mail Transfer Protocol), DNS (Domain Name System), TELNET (Teletype Network), FTP (File Transfer Protocol), and TFTP (Trivial File Transfer Protocol).

Electronic mail (i.e., email) is a network application. It uses the SMTP. An email application consists of user agent (e.g., web-based Gmail on a browser, Gmail App in a smartphone, Microsoft Outlook, Apple mail), mail servers, and simple mail transfer protocol.

Let us understand the working of email application with an example shown in **Figure 4.11**. As shown in **Figure 4.11**, User **A** wants to send an email to user **B.** User **A** with its user agent writes an email content and composes it. The email goes to the A's mail server. Then A's mail server transmits the emails to the B's mail server, where the user B mailbox is present. B's mail server puts the email in the B's mailbox. When user B wants to retrieve the email, it gets from its mail server. User agent uses SMTP or HTTP to send a message to its mail server. The communication between the mail servers use the SMTP. To retrieve the email from its mailbox, user B uses its user agent to get the email using IMAP (Internet mail access protocol) or HTTP (hypertext transfer protocol).

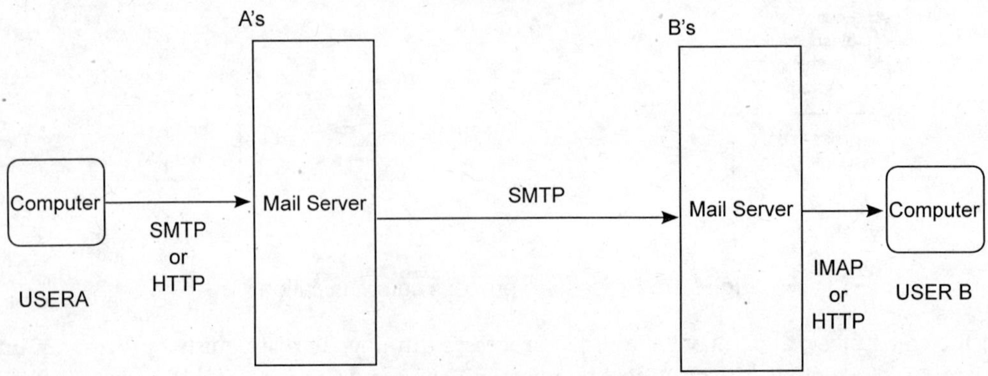

Fig. 4.11: Mail transmission

4.4 SIMPLE MAIL TRANSFER PROTOCOL (SMTP)

SMTP is the core of the mail application. It is mainly used in mail transfer between mail servers. A user agent may also use SMTP to send email to its mail server. The client SMTP (which is executing on the A's mail server) establishes a TCP connection on port number 25 to the server SMTP (which is executing on the B's mail server). It performs SMTP handshaking. In this handshaking, client SMTP shares the sender's and recipient's email address. After this handshaking, client SMTP sends the messages to the server SMTP over transmission control protocol, which provides reliable transmission service.

We have already seen a network application sends/receives data through the socket interface. A socket interface is a place where an application gets the transport layer services. A socket is a special file (in the terminology of Unix). Let us understand through an example how a simple mail transfer protocol (i.e., a set of rules) is used to transmit a message from user A to user B. The data/massage are going to be written on a socket file adhering to the SMTP rules. Let the mail server hostname of user A is abcd.in, and the mail server hostname of user B is wxyz.edu. The client SMTP (which is running at the abcd.in) and server SMTP (which is running at wxyz.edu). A TCP connection will be made between client SMTP and server SMTP. After the TCP connection is made, the socket file at the client SMTP mail server and server SMTP mail server are shown **in Table 4. 3.** Each client and server SMTP write and read from their own socket file.

Table 4.3: Mail transmission between mail servers using SMTP

Client SMTP mail server abcd.in		Server SMTP mail server wxyz.edu
Socket file HELO abcd.in MAIL FROM:<A@abcd.in> RCPT TO:<B@wxyz.edu>		Socket file 250 Hello abcd.in 250 A@abcd.in Sender ok 250 B@wxyz.in Recipient ok
DATA		
		354 Enter mail, end with "." on a line
How are you? What are you doing? I am learning computer network .		
		250 Message Accepted
QUIT		
		221 wxyz.edu closing connection
Operating System	Internet	Operating System
CPU, Memory, I/O, Disk		CPU, Memory, I/O, Disk

Here, the client SMTP writes on its socket; then, it is transmitted through the network to the server SMTP socket. Server SMTP reads the data from its socket, which is sent by the client SMTP. When server SMTP writes on its socket, then it is transmitted through the network. The client SMTP reads data from its socket, which is sent by the server SMTP. In the above example, the SMTP commands are HELO, MAILFROM, RCPT TO, DATT, DATA, QUIT. SMTP protocol is defined in RFC [5321]. All commands can be seen from RFC [5321].

4.4.1 Internet Mail Access Protocol

A user can retrieve email from the mailbox which resides on the mail server. A user uses the user agent, which uses Internet Mail Access Protocol (IMAP) (defined in RFC 3501) or HTTP (in the case of web-based email, for example, Gmail). SMTP is a push protocol. SMTP is not used for retrieving email. HTTP is a protocol used for web applications.

4.5 DOMAIN NAME SYSTEM (DNS)

A host can be identified by its hostname, for example, www.google.com, www.yahoo.com. This kind of mnemonic name is easily memorable by humans. A host is also identified by an IP address. Human prefers mnemonic hostnames, and router prefers IP addresses. A directory service is required to map the hostname to an IP address. Domain Name System is an application layer protocol that runs over UDP (uses the port number 53) and distributed database implemented in a hierarchy of servers. DNS also provides functionalities, like host aliasing, mail server aliasing, and load distribution, along with translating hostname to an IP address. DNS is a complex system; this book only talks about the overview of DNS.

A very simple design can be a single DNS server machine that maintains all the mappings. But this design has many problems, such as single point failure, cannot handle all the requests from all over the world, which may be the order of hundreds of millions (i.e., 10^8), high delay, and maintenance issues. Therefore, Domain Name System is implemented in a distributed fashion and established worldwide. The DNS servers are categorised into three, namely (i) root, (ii) top-level domain, and (iii) authoritative.

There are 13 different root DNS servers that exist. The management of the root servers are done by Internet Assigned Numbers Authority (IANA) and twelve organizations. Root DNS server contains information of the top-level domain servers. To ensure the availability and reliability, there are more than one thousand root server instances are installed all over the world.

Top-Level Domain (TLD) servers are server machines corresponding to top-level domain, such as com, net, edu, org, gov, uk, fr, ca, and so on. The network infrastructure for supporting top-level domain is complex. The TLD servers maintains information related to the authoritative DNS servers. Authoritative DNS servers contain the DNS records. Many large companies and universities maintain their own authoritative server. Some may host their DNS data on some authoritative DNS server service provider by paying some fee. A hierarchy of DNS servers (partially) is shown in **Figure 4.12.**

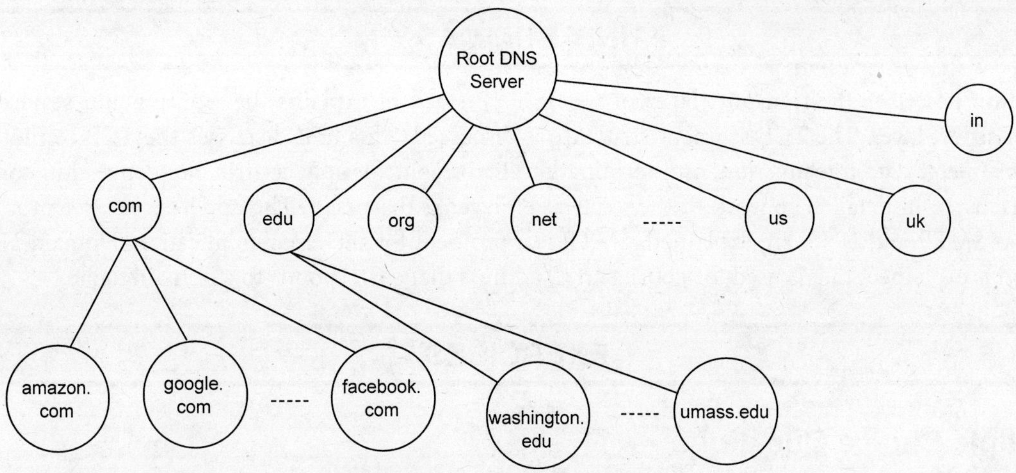

Fig. 4.12: Domain name system

An Internet Service Provider (ISP) also installs a local DNS server, known as default name server). If an end system is connected to an ISP for Internet, the ISP tells the IP address of its local DNS server.

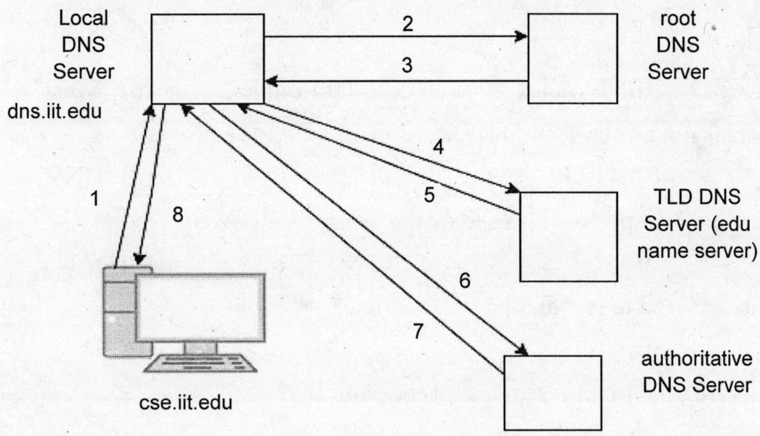

Fig. 4.13: DNS example

To understand the working of the DNS, take an example that a host cse.iit.edu wants to know the IP address of host merry.cse.nit.edu. The host cse.iit.edu transmits a request to its local DNS server dns. iit.edu, the local DNS server transmits a request to the root server, the root server replies the IP address of TLD DNS server to the local DNS server. The local DNS server again transmits a request to the TLD DNS server, and the TLD DNS server replies the IP address of authoritative server to the local DNS server. The local DNS server again transmits a request to the authoritative server that replies the IP address of the desired host merry.cse.nit.edu to the local DNS server. The local DNS server now replies to the host cse.iit.edu. The process of communication of DNS servers is shown in **Figure 4.13.**

If you want to enter your DNS record (i.e., the domain name of your newly opened company), you can register the domain name to the **registrar** (it is a commercial entity, it verifies the uniqueness of the domain name and make entry into the DNS database). There are many registrars. These registrars are accredited by Internet Corporation for Assigned Names and Numbers (ICANN).

UNIT SUMMARY

This unit describes the transport layer of the TCP/IP stack. It explains the working and services of the transport layer. The TCP segment structure is discussed. This unit discusses the TCP connection establishment, data transmission, and termination. Error control, flow control, are congestion control are discussed in detail. The work of the application layer is discussed. The application layer protocol, such as SMTP and DNS, are explained. SMTP is a protocol for the email application. Domain Name System is explained, that is used for getting an IP address that corresponds to a domain name.

EXERCISES

Multiple Choice Questions

1. From the protocol given in the options, choose which of these uses TCP?
   (a) DHCP (b) FTP and SMTP (c) TFTP (d) DHCP and TFTP
2. Application layer protocol given in the options, which of these uses UDP?
   (a) FTP (b) HTTP (c) SMTP (d) DNS
3. TCP supports?
   (a) Half-duplex (b) Simplex (c) Full-duplex. (d) None
4. Which protocol is not an application layer protocol?
   (a) HTTP (b) FTP (c) TCP (d) DNS
5. Which application layer protocol is used by the World Wide Web?
   (a) IMAP (b) HTTP (c) FTP (d) SMTP
6. How many bits are used to represent a port number?
   (a) 4 (b) 8 (c) 32 (d) 16
7. How many bits are used to represent a sequence number?
   (a) 16 (b) 32 (c) 64 (d) 8
8. The port number used by SMTP is?
   (a) 23 (b) 21 (c) 80 (d) 25
9. Which one is used as a port number by DNS?
   (a) 20 (b) 53 (c) 443 (d) 22
10. What is the purpose of the SYN flag in the TCP segment?
   (a) To synchronize sequence number (b) close connection
   (c) send data (d) none

ANSWERS															
1.	(b)	2.	(d)	3.	(c)	4.	(c)	5.	(b)	6.	(d)	7.	(b)	8.	(d)
9.	(b)	10.	(a)												

Questions (Short Answer)

1. Differentiate between connectionless and connection-oriented transmission?
2. Explain three-way handshaking for TCP connection establishment?
3. Explain how TCP terminates a connection?
4. What is error control, and how is it achieved by TCP?
5. What is flow control, and how is it achieved by TCP?
6. What is an application layer protocol?
7. What is a port number, and what is its purpose?
8. Describe the client and server.
9. What is Internet Mail Access Protocol?
10. Explain the domain name system?

Questions (Long Answer)

1. Describe the structure of a TCP segment.
2. Describe the working of the congestion control algorithm.
3. Explain how reliability is achieved by transmission control protocol.
4. Explain the working of the Simple Mail Transfer Protocol.

PRACTICAL

Aim - 1

Look at various networking devices in the lab. Explore the functionalities and working of these devices.

1. NIC
2. Hub
3. Switch
4. Router
5. Wi-Fi access point.

Aim – 2

Look at the specifications of the above networking devices of various companies on the Internet and find out the differences.

KNOW MORE

WWW and HTTP

World Wide Web, also termed the Web, is a network application invented by Tim Berners-Lee. It is an application that has a very high impact on public life. It makes available content on demand. The Web and its protocol provide a platform through which anyone can provide their content accessible all over the world at a very low cost. Web-based applications like YouTube, web-based email, and most applications on the Internet use the Web and its protocol as a platform. HyperText Transfer Protocol (HTTP) is an application layer protocol for WWW. A web page is a document that contains files (also termed objects). An object can be HTML (HyperText Markup Language) file, CSS (Cascading Style Sheet) file, image file, and video file. An object is addressable through an URL (Uniform Resource Locator). An URL is the hostname of the server machine (on which objects are stored) along with the object location path. HTTP is implemented by a client program as well as by a server program. Web browsers (e.g., Firefox, Chrome, Internet explorer) implement the client side of HyperText Transfer Protocol. Web Servers (e.g., Apache, Nginx, Lighttpd, Microsoft internet information server) implement the server side of HTTP. Web server houses the web objects which are accessible using URLs. The web client and web server communicate by sending/receiving HTTP messages. HTTP defines the format of a message for the communication between the web client and web server.

REFERENCES AND SUGGESTED READINGS

1. Andrew S. Tanenbaum, Computer Networks, 5th Edition, PHI
2. W. Richard Stevens, TCP/IP Illustrated, Volume-1, Addision Wesley, Second Edition
3. James F. Kurose and Keith W. Ross, Computer Networking: A Top–Down Approach, Pearson, Eight Edition
4. Behrouz A. Forouzan and Firouz Mosharraf, Computer Networks: A Top-Down Approach, Mc Graw Hill Education, Special Indian Edition 2012
5. William Stalling, Computer Networking with Internet Protocols and Technology, Pearson Education, First Edition

Dynamic QR Code for Further Reading

5 Networking Devices and Network Management System

UNIT SPECIFICS

Through this unit, we discuss the following aspects:

- Network Interface Card;
- Hub;
- Switch;
- Router;
- Wi-Fi Device;
- Network Management System;
- SNMP.

The unit explains the network management through working of networking devices. Network interface card working is explained. The functionality of hub, switch, and router are discussed in detail along with the services they offer. The discussion on wireless devices is taken up next. Network management system and its protocol - SNMP is explained. This unit contains questions for practice. This also provides references for further reading. There is a "Know More" section carefully designed that gives supplementary information based on the context of this unit. A laboratory task is included to get acquainted with a network simulator. A laboratory task is added to configure a wired and wireless local area network.

RATIONALE

This unit on network devices helps students to get an understanding of the working of the network. The working of a network interface card, hub, switch, router, and wi-fi device is explained. This will pave the way for a clear understanding of the configuration of these devices. The network management concepts and protocols are helpful in maintaining and monitoring the network.

PRE-REQUISITES

This unit requires Unit 1, Unit 2, Unit 3, and Unit 4 of this book.

UNIT OUTCOMES

The six outcomes of this unit are given below:

U5-O1: Description of network interface card

U5-O2: Description of a hub

U5-O3: Explanation of switch

U5-O4: Description of a router

U5-O5: Description of Wi-Fi devices

U5-O6: Explanation of network management and SNMP

Unit-5 Outcomes	EXPECTED MAPPING WITH COURSE OUTCOMES (1- Weak Correlation; 2- Medium correlation; 3- Strong Correlation)				
	CO-1	CO-2	CO-3	CO-4	CO-5
U5-O1	2	3	3	3	3
U5-O2	2	3	2	2	2
U5-O3	2	3	3	3	3
U5-O4	2	2	2	3	3
U5-O5	2	2	3	3	3
U5-O6	2	2	2	2	2

5.1 NETWORKING DEVICES

A computer network is composed of many networking connecting devices. These devices are, namely, network interface cards, hubs, switches, routers, and wireless connecting devices. The function and working of these devices are different. These devices serve different purposes in the transmission of data in the network. The structure and functioning of these devices are discussed in the subsequent sections.

5.2 NETWORK INTERFACE CARD

A network interface card, also termed as a network adapter, network interface controller, or network card, is a device by which a computer is connected to a network. It is a hardware circuit board installed in a computer. It is an essential device that enables an end system for connection to a network. In modern days, a computer system generally has a network card on its motherboard. The network card may be built on the dedicated chip and connected to the computer. A network card implements the data link layer functionalities, such as framing, link access, and error detection. Some of these functionalities are implemented in hardware, and some of these are implemented as software. The network card implements data link layer standards, such as Ethernet or WiFi. NIC can be for wired or for wireless connection. Network card works at physical and data link layers both. A network adapter connects a computing device to a network using a cable or wirelessly. Server machine motherboards generally have more than one network card. To configure a network adapter a software (termed as a device driver) is installed on the computer. Network card uses the techniques, such as polling, or interrupt driven I/O, to indicate that a packet is available to transfer.

A NIC consists of a controller, boot ROM socket, port for cable, bus interface, and LED indicator. The controller is the main component that performs the functions provided by NIC. The boot ROM provides support for connecting a diskless workstation. NIC port (e.g., RJ45, AUI port, BNC port for ethernet cable, coaxial cable, and optical cable) is the place where a cable is connected. For a wireless network, NIC has an antenna that uses the radio wave the communication. LED indicator indicates the working status of the NIC. NIC supports the data transmission speed of 10 and 100 Mbps, 1, 10, 25, 40, and 100 Gbps.

5.3 HUB (REPEATER)

Hub is also known as a repeater. Hub works at the physical layer only. Data transmission is carried out through a medium (wired or wireless). Electromagnetic waves carry the data signal traveling through the medium. Due to attenuation, the data signal may be corrupted after traveling a fixed distance in the medium. If a data signal (before it is corrupted or too weak) reaches to a hub, it is regenerated at the hub and then forwarded. A hub simply regenerates the data signal and forwards them.

In the bus topology of Ethernet LAN, a hub (repeater) is used to extend the range (length) of the coaxial cable (i.e., to overcome the limitation of length). In the star topology of Ethernet LAN, a hub (as a multiport device) is used as a connecting point for end systems. A hub forwards the regenerated data signal to all the ports except the port to which the data signal is received. A hub does ***not have filtering capability***. As shown in **Figure 5.1,** if host E sends a data signal, the data signal is regenerated and forwarded to A, B, C, & D.

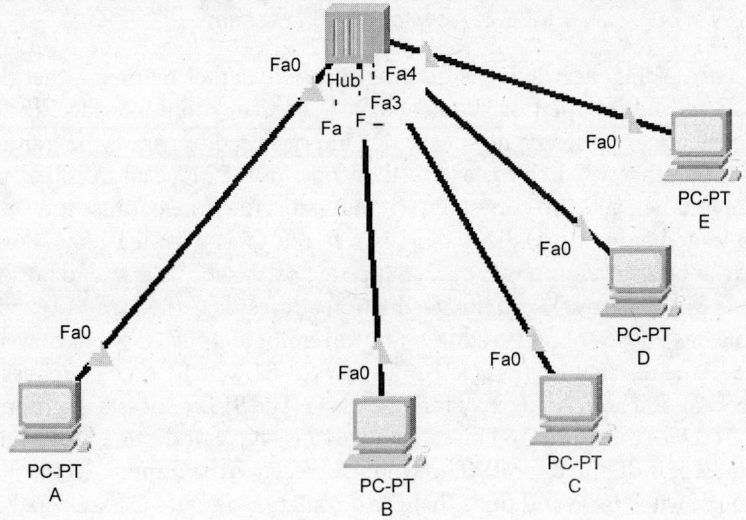

Fig. 5.1: A hub connected with five computers

5.4 SWITCH

Link layer switch is a device that works up to the data link layer. This device performs the regeneration of data signal (i.e., the task of a physical layer) and filtering & forwarding by reading the frame header (i.e., MAC address of source and destination). Link-layer switch is a transparent device that a host/router is unaware of switch in the network. It means that no packet is addressed to any switch. It is a plug-and-play device; there is not any configuration requirement by the network administrator. A switch interface has a buffer to store frames.

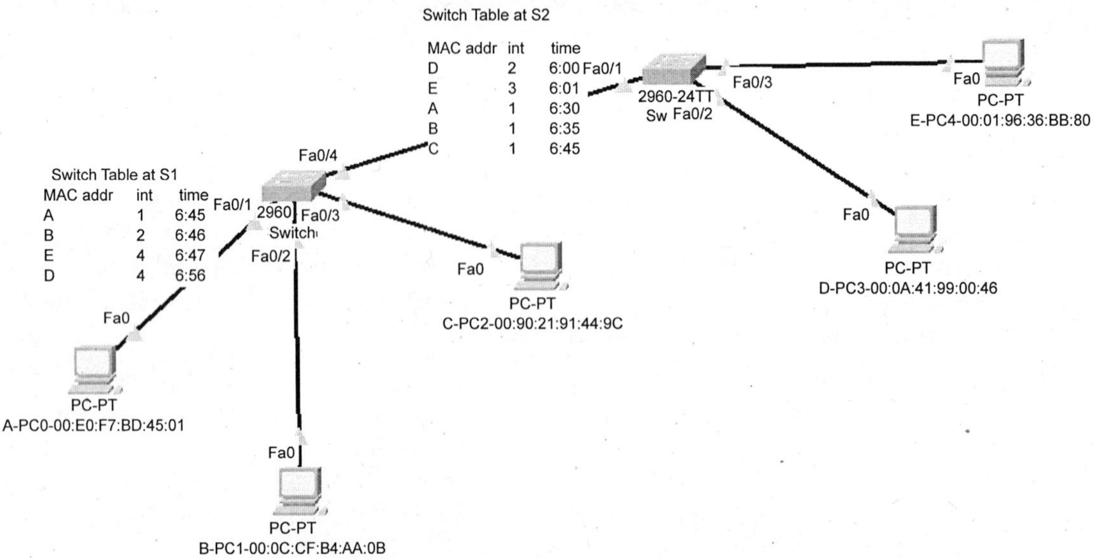

Fig. 5.2: A switch working scenario

Filtering and Forwarding: A switch has filtering capability. Filtering means that the switch decides whether a frame should be dropped or should be forwarded to some interface. If a frame has to be forwarded to some interface, the switch decides which interface and transmits the frame to that interface. This is termed as forwarding. A switch has a table that contains the MAC address (i.e., physical address), (ii) switch interface number, and (iii) timestamp (it maintains the time because it deletes the entry after some time period, called aging time). This table is referred to as a switch table. For instance, let the switching table entries be as given in **Figure 5.2.** Suppose host A sends a frame to host C, i.e., the sender address is A (i.e., A's MAC address), and the destination address is C (i.e., C's MAC address). In Figure 5.2, the switch table has entries of MAC address; however, for simplicity, we have written the name of the host itself. The frame reaches at interface 1 of the switch S1. The S1 now searches in its switch table for the MAC address of C. There is no entry for address C. The S1 broadcasts the frame to its interfaces 2, 3, and 4. Host B receives the frame and discards it (because it is not destined for it). Host C receives it and accepts it (because it is destined for it). The switch S2 receives the frame at its interface 1. The switch S2 now searches in its switch table and finds that the destination address C is associated with interface 1 (the same interface at which the frame is received). Hence, Switch S2 will filter the frame by discarding it. Suppose host A sends a frame to host E. The frame will be received at switch S1 at interface 1. The switch S1 searches in its switch table and finds that the interface 4. The switch S1 forwards the frame to interface 4. The switch S2 receives the frame at interface 1. The switch S2 searches in its switch table and finds interface 3. The switch S2 forwards the frame to interface 3, and then the frame is received at host E.

A switch learns the entries of the switch table without the intervention of a network administrator or a configuration protocol. The switch learns the entries from the source address of the frame. For instance, let us take the switch table as empty. If host A sends a frame to host D. Switch S1 makes an entry in its switch table for host A and interface 1 (because the frame is received at interface 1 of S1 and the source address in the frame is the MAC address of A). Similarly, at switch S2, an entry will be added for host A and interface 1 of switch S2 in the S2's switch table because the frame is received at interface 1 of S2, and the frame has the source physical address of host A.

The purpose of the time stamp is that after some time (termed as aging time) the entry is deleted and learned again. That is used to deal with if an end system is removed, then entry has to be removed from the switch automatically.

5.5 ROUTER

A router is a device that interconnects networks. It works at (i) the physical layer (regenerates the data signal), (ii) the data link layer (investigates the source and destination physical address), and (iii) the network layer (checks the IP addresses). Each interface of a router has a physical address as well as an IP address. If a packet is received at a router's input port, the router acts only on that packet which has a destination physical address the same as the router interface physical address. A router changes the source and destination physical address of the packet when it forwards. A router has input ports (interfaces), output ports (interfaces), switching fabric, and a router processor, as shown in **Figure 5.3**.

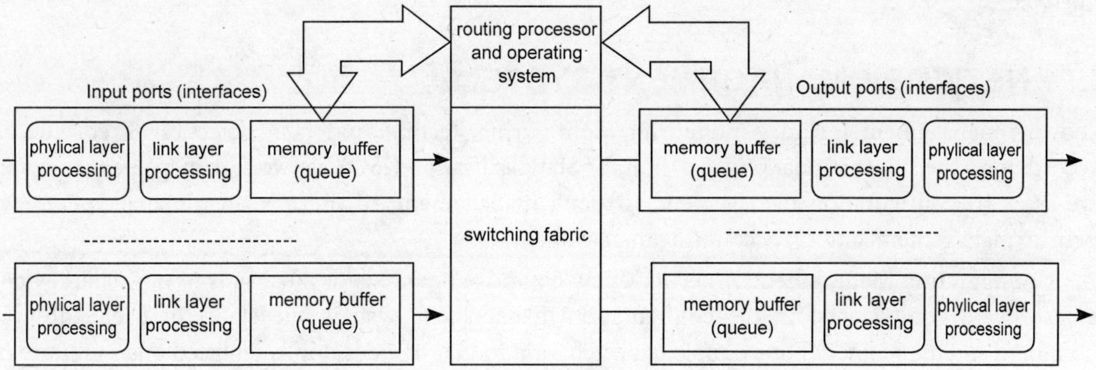

Fig. 5.3: An abstract view of a router

Input port (interface): At this port, a router receives a signal and performs the physical layer processing, and constructs the bits (that is, the packet). After this, link layer processing performs the error checking on the frame. If the frame is correct and dedicated to this interface, the frame is decapsulated and is become ready for the network layer processing by the routing processor. If the frame is erroneous or not dedicated for this port (interface), it is discarded. The input port also has a memory buffer (termed as a queue) to store the packets because the router may be busy processing some other packet.

Routing processor: It takes the packet from the input port (interface) and finds the next hop IP address by using the destination IP address in the packet. The router also finds the output port (interface) to which the packet is going to be sent. This is done by looking into the forwarding table. Modern development moves the routing processor to the ports.

Switching fabric: It performs the task of moving the packet from the input port (queue) to the output port (queue). Earlier, when the task of a router was done by a computer, the computer's memory was utilized for the task of switching fabric. However, recent development built many switching fabrics, such as crossbar switch, banyan switch, and batcher-banyan switch.

Output port (interface): It stores the packet in the output queue (memory buffer). After this, the link layer processing performs the encapsulation and makes a frame. After this, the physical layer processing takes the frame and creates a data signal and transmits it on the medium.

5.6 WI-FI DEVICE

A Wi-Fi device is a wireless device (i.e., to make a network, it does not require a wired medium). Most laptops have a wireless network adapter (i.e., a wireless network interface card). This wireless network adapter implements the IEEE 802.11 standard. The wireless adapter enables devices (e.g., laptops, mobile phones, etc.) to connect with a wireless network. Wireless Access Point (WAP), also termed as an access point, is a device that enables to connect a device (which has a wireless adapter in it) to a wired network. It is used to create a wireless network within the existing wired network. WAP provides a connection point to wireless users. WAP is directly connected to the wired local area network. In simple words, a device having a wireless network adapter is connected to an access point, and the access point is connected to a wired local area network through a switch or a router. A wireless router does the function of a wireless access point and router both. It integrates both functionalities in a single device. It works in a wired LAN, wireless LAN alone, or a mix of both. The working of a wireless LAN is discussed in unit 2 of this book.

5.7 NETWORK MANAGEMENT SYSTEM

Network management includes monitoring, configuring, testing, and fault detection & correction. According to the International Organization for Standardisation (ISO), network management includes five areas (i) configuration management, (ii) fault management, (ii) performance management, (iv) security management, and (v) accounting management.

Configuration Management: A network may comprise hundreds or thousands of physical devices and software components. In the configuration management system, the status of each entity is monitored and maintained. For example, a switch, or a router, or a desktop is replaced due to failure or some reason. Application software may be updated. The configuration management system takes care of reconfiguring and documenting. The reconfiguration deals with hardware reconfiguration, software reconfiguration, and user accounts reconfiguration. Hardware reconfiguration maintains all the issues related to the hardware component of the network. For example, a router may be moved from one network to other. A new desktop may be added. A subnetwork may be added or removed. Specialized and well-trained personnel are required for hardware reconfiguration. It cannot be automated. Software reconfiguration takes care of the changes to software. Most of the software reconfiguration are automated to a large extent. User account reconfiguration takes care of user privileges. For example, a user may have only read permission for a file but may have read and write permission for another file. User account reconfiguration can be automated to some extent. For the hardware, software, and user accounts reconfiguration, the subsequent changes must be recorded. The hardware documentation is recorded in the form of a map (which contains the physical location of devices and logical connection among them) and recorded specification of each device, such as warranty, serial number, vendor details, time of purchase, etc. Software reconfiguration documentation maintains the version number of the software, time of installation, license agreement, etc. For the user account configuration, the most operating system provides a utility that allows user account documentation.

Fault Management: A network may have hundreds or thousands of physical and software components. To work a network properly, each component of the network must operate properly. Fault management deals with detecting a fault, isolating a fault, correcting a fault, and recording the fault.

Performance Management: This monitors and controls the network to ensure that the network is working efficiently. Performance is measured using measurable quantities, such as response time, throughput, traffic, and capacity. SNMP (Simple Network Management Protocol) is primarily used for performance management.

Security Management: Security management deals with access control to network devices according to a pre-defined policy. Encryption, decryption, and authentication are used for security management.

Account Management: Account management is basically accounting for the individual user, departments, divisions, and so on through charges. Charges are not necessarily a cash transfer. Accounting management is used to prevent users from monopolizing limited network resources. It is also used for short-term and long-term planning of the network.

5.7.1 Simple Network Management Protocol

SNMP is used for network management using TCP/IP protocol suite. SNMP is an application layer protocol. It can monitor and control devices made by different manufacturers. There are two entities, namely, a manager and an agent. The manager (usually a program running on a host) controls agents, as shown in **Figure 5.4**.

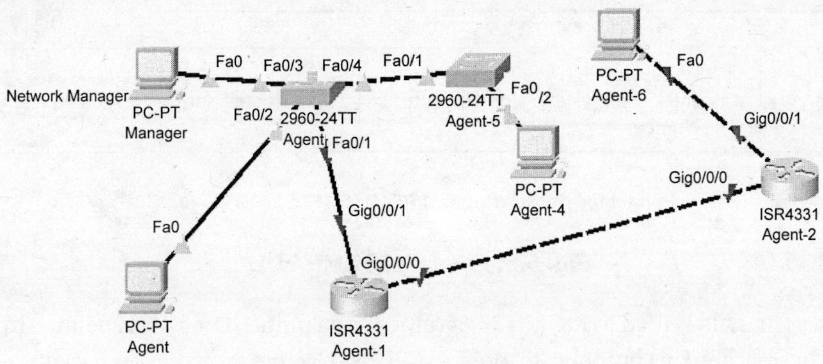

Fig. 5.4: A network manager and agents

An agent can be any device, such as a desktop, server, switch, or router. Agents are basically managed devices by a manager. The manager executes the SNMP client process. An agent executes the SNMP server process. Network management is done through the interaction between manager and agent (that is, request and response between them). A request is commonly a query to fetch or modify (a set of new values of certain variables, i.e., objects). An agent simply receives a request and acts accordingly, either reply or modify. An agent has stored the performance information in a database and sends these information to the manager on request. For example, a router stores the information number of packets received and forwarded. When a manager requests this information, the agent replies this. The manager can use this value to find whether the router is congested or not by comparing the number of received and forwarded packets. A manager can also reboot a router by setting the reboot counter to 0. An agent can also send a warning message (also known as a trap) to the manager. Basically, the management is carried out by the manager using the status information of agents by performing the action, that is, resetting values in the agent's database. SNMP uses two protocols, namely (i) Structure of Management

Information (SMI) and (ii) Management Information Base (MIB), for the management task. SNMP defines the format of a packet that is used for communication between the manager and agent. SNMP is used to fetch the values of the objects defined in an agent. SNMP modifies the status of a variable (i.e., the value of the variable) if required. It creates statistics and interprets them with the help of other software tools.

SNMP version 3 defines the PDU (Protocol Data Unit). These PDUs are eight, namely (i) GetRequest, (ii) GetNextRequest, (iii) GetBulkRequest, (iv) SetRequest, (v) Response, (vi) Trap, (vii) InformRequest, and (viii) Report. The format of SNMP PDU is shown in **Figure 5.5**.

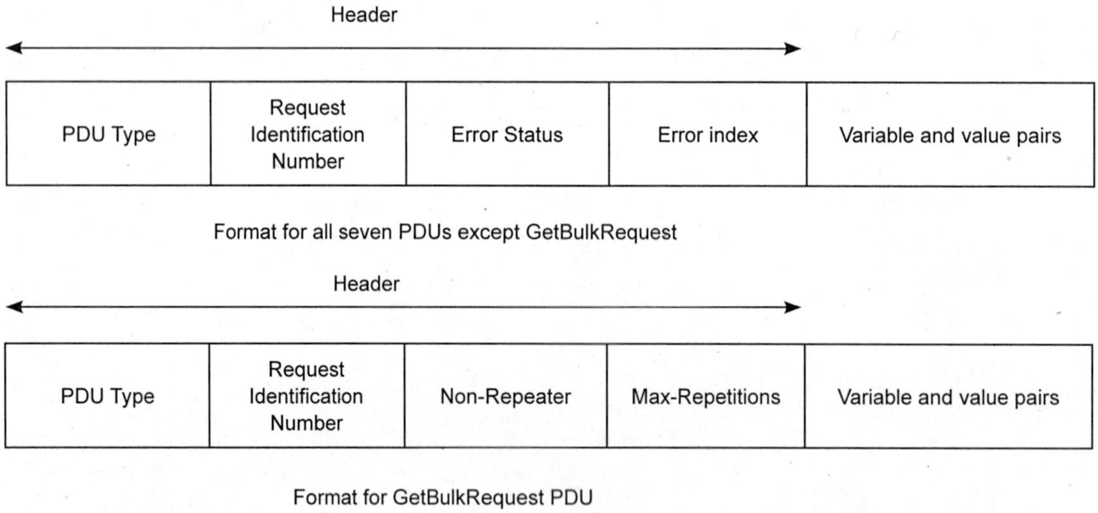

Fig. 5.5: Format of SNMP PDU

PDU Type: This field is used to identify the protocol data unit. There is a predefined integer number for each PDU. In a packet, this number is stored in this field, so the receiver of a packet can identify it.

Request Identification Number: This field stores a sequence number that is used to match a request to their response. In response PDU, the agent repeats the same sequence number.

For all the request messages error status field and error index field are set to zero.

Error Status: This field is used only in response PDU. It shows the types of error at the agent. For example, zero is used to represent no error, 4 is used to represent that value cannot be modified because it is read-only.

Error Index: It is an offset to indicate which variable is causing the error.

Variable and Value Pair: It is a list of variables and corresponding values. In the request PDUs, the values are null. If the manager wants to set it, the manager puts the desired value to the corresponding variable.

Non-Repeaters: Get Bulk Request PDU uses this field. This field indicates non-repeating variables at the start of the variable-value pair list.

Max-Repetitions: This field is also used in the GetBulkRequest PDU. This field defines the iteration required to read all the repeating objects.

At the transport layer, the SNMP communication uses the UDP (User Datagram Protocol), and well-known port numbers 161 (at the agent) and 162 (at the manager).

SMI (Structure of Management Information): It defines rules to name objects (variables), type of objects, and to encode the objects and values. A general rule is required because one does not know the architecture of the computer or device that sends, receives, or stores these values.

Management Information Base (MIB): MIB creates the objects and their relationship among the objects. The objects are categorized into groups, such as sys, if, at, ip, icmp, tcp, and udp.

UNIT SUMMARY

This unit explains the working of the networking devices that are used to create a network. A hub is a simple device that is used to extend a network and connects more end systems. A switch is a device that extends a network transparently. A switch has a filtering capability that helps to stop the flooding of packets and improves the bandwidth utilization of the network. A router, a device, is used to communicate among different networks. A router takes a datagram packet and forwards it to the output interface, which leads to the destination on the basis of the forwarding table. Routing protocols are used to create a forwarding table. A network interface card is a device that makes a computer system connected to a network. This device implements the data link layer standards. Ethernet and Wi-Fi standards are implemented on the network card. It can be wired or wireless. This unit also explains the network management concept and its protocol.

EXERCISES

Multiple Choice Questions

1. Which of the following does not have filtering capability?
   (a) switch (b) hub (c) router (d) none
2. Which one is not a connecting device?
   (a) router (b) hub (c) switch (d) end system
3. In the given options, choose a device that is not an end system.
   (a) Mobile smartphone (b) Laptop
   (c) Router (d) Web Server
4. Device which works at the physical layer only?
   (a) Laptop (b) switch (c) router (d) hub
5. Device which works at the physical and data link layer both but not at the network layer?
   (a) Desktop (b) Router (c) Switch (d) Hub
6. Device which works at all three physical, data link, and network layers?
   (a) Router (b) Hub (c) Switch (d) None
7. ------ Protocol is used at the data link layer?
   (a) POP (b) Ethernet (c) TCP (d) BGP

8. ----- Port is used by SNMP?
   (a) 20 and 21 (b) 443 (c) 161 and 162 (d) 520
9. ------- Protocol is used at a router?
   (a) RIP (b) OSPF (c) BGP (d) All
10. ------ Protocol is used for network management?
    (a) FTP (b) HTTP (c) SMTP (d) SNMP

ANSWERS															
1.	(b)	2.	(d)	3.	(c)	4.	(d)	5.	(c)	6.	(a)	7.	(b)	8.	(c)
9.	(d)	10.	(d)												

Questions (Short Answer)

1. Describe the role of network connecting devices?
2. Describe the network interface card and its role?
3. What is the purpose of a hub, and how does it work?
4. What is the task of a switching table?
5. Describe filtering and forwarding in a switch device?
6. Describe the components of a router?
7. Describe a Wi-Fi device.
8. Write the role of a network management system.
9. What is the purpose of a simple network management protocol?
10. Differentiate between hub, switch, and router?

Questions (Long Answer)

1. Explain the working of a switch.
2. Describe the working of a router.
3. Write a note on simple network management protocol.
4. Explain the network management system.

PRACTICAL

Aim -1

Network simulation tool: Cisco Packet Tracer is a network simulation tool.

(a) Go to the website www.netacad.com download the cisco packet tracer and install it on your desktop or laptop.

(b) Explore the end devices, routers, switches, hubs, and wireless devices in the simulator.

(c) Explore Cables - straight through, crossover, and automatic default connection.

Aim -2

Setting up a small, wired LAN in the Lab

Step 1: Take a switch

Step 2: Take 5 PCs

Step 3: Connects these through the straight-through cable

Step 4: Click on PC0, you will see a setting window. Click on config, and click on FastEthernet0. You will see a static IPv4 address and subnet mask setting. Provide an IP address 192.168.10.2 and subnet mask 255.255.255.0 and close the window. **Figure 5.6** show these settings.

Step 5: Similarly, for the other 4 PCs, configure the given IP address and subnet mask

192.168.10.3	255.255.255.0	for PC -1
192.168.10.4	255.255.255.0	for PC -2
192.168.10.5	255.255.255.0	for PC -3
192.168.10.6	255.255.255.0	for PC -4

Step 6: Choose a simple PDU message, click on PC0, and again click on PC 3. You will see that the message is transmitted successfully. There is a simulation play button on the right side. Click on that button and see the visuals. Look in **Figure 5.6** given below to take help.

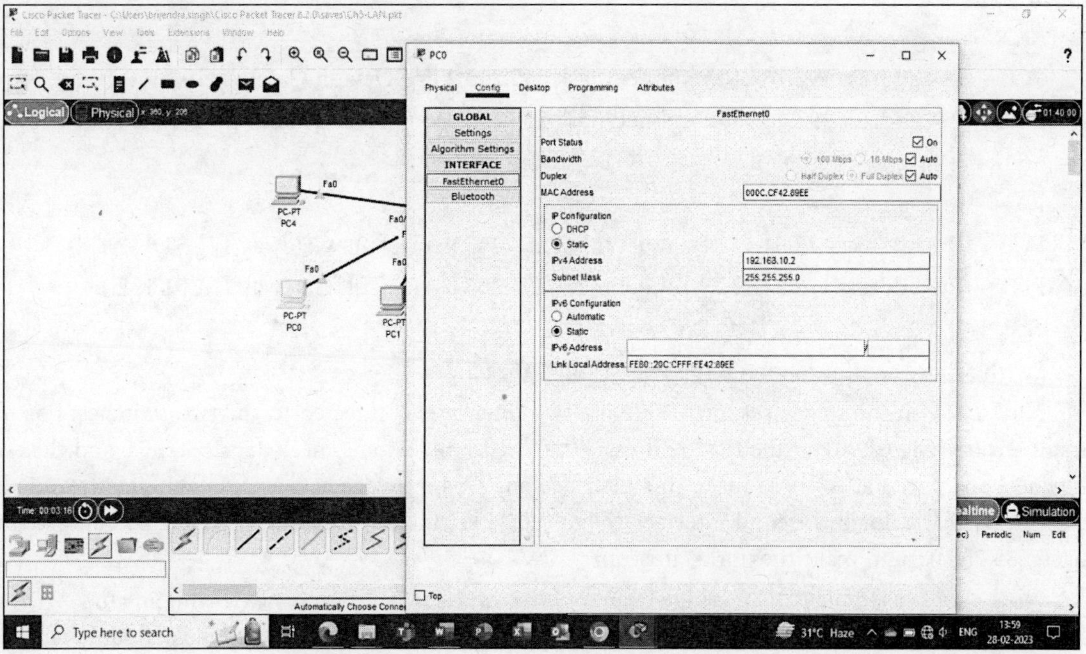

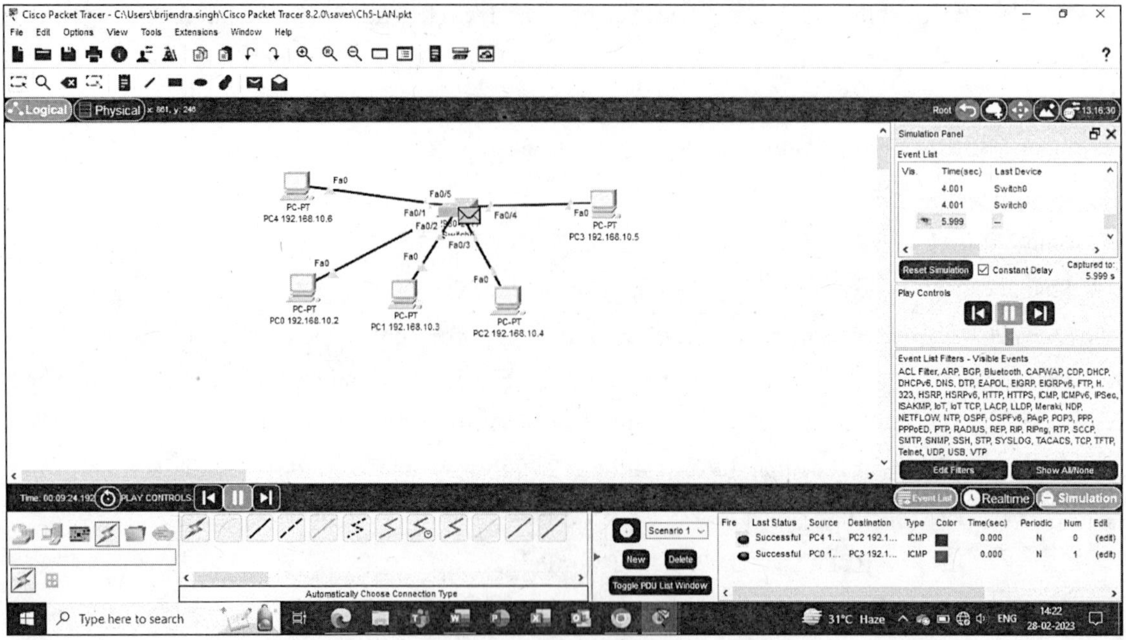

Fig. 5.6: IP address and subnet mask setting

Similarly, take one router and two switches. Connect each switch with 2 PCs. Furthermore, connect the switches to the router. Here, we are creating two LANs and interconnecting these two LANs with a router.

LAN – A:

PC0 – IPv4 address 192.168.10.2 subnet mask 255.255.255.0 Default Gateway 192.168.10.1

PC1 – IPv4 address 192.168.10.3 subnet mask 255.255.255.0 Default Gateway 192.168.10.1

LAN – B

PC2 – IPv4 address 172.31.132.2 subnet mask 255.255.0.0 Default Gateway 171.31.132.1

PC3 – IPv4 address 172.31.132.3 subnet mask 255.255.0.0 Default Gateway 171.31.132.1

Set the above configuration on the PCs, as in **Figure 5.7**.

Now, click on the router setting. There are two interfaces connected to the two switches. For the first interface (Gig/0/0/0) set the IPv4 address 192.168.10.1 and subnet mask 255.255.255.0 and click on the checkbox port status 'on' to make this interface on. This interface acts as a default gateway for the LAN-A. Similarly, for the second interface (Gig0/0/0/1) set the IPv4 address 172.31.132.1 and subnet mask 255.255.0.0 and make the port status 'on'.

Now, choose a simple PDU message from tools bar and send it from one PC belonging to LAN A to the PC belonging to LAN B. Send many messages among the PCs. If the message fails, double-click on the 'Fire' again. It will resend the message.

Click on PC, then click on the desktop, then click on the command prompt. Execute ping and ipconfig command. **Figure 5.8** and **Figure 5.9** are given below for your help.

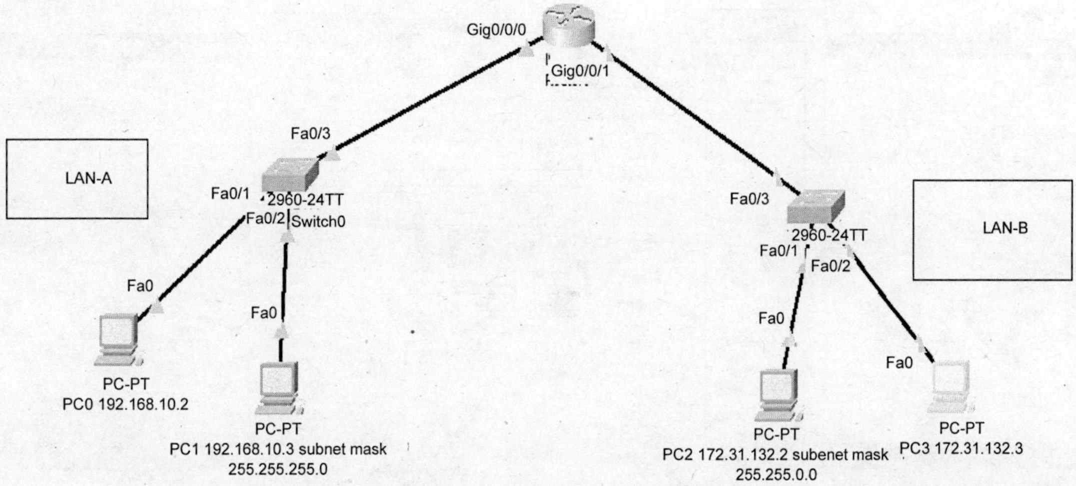

Fig. 5.7: Two LAN interconnection through a router

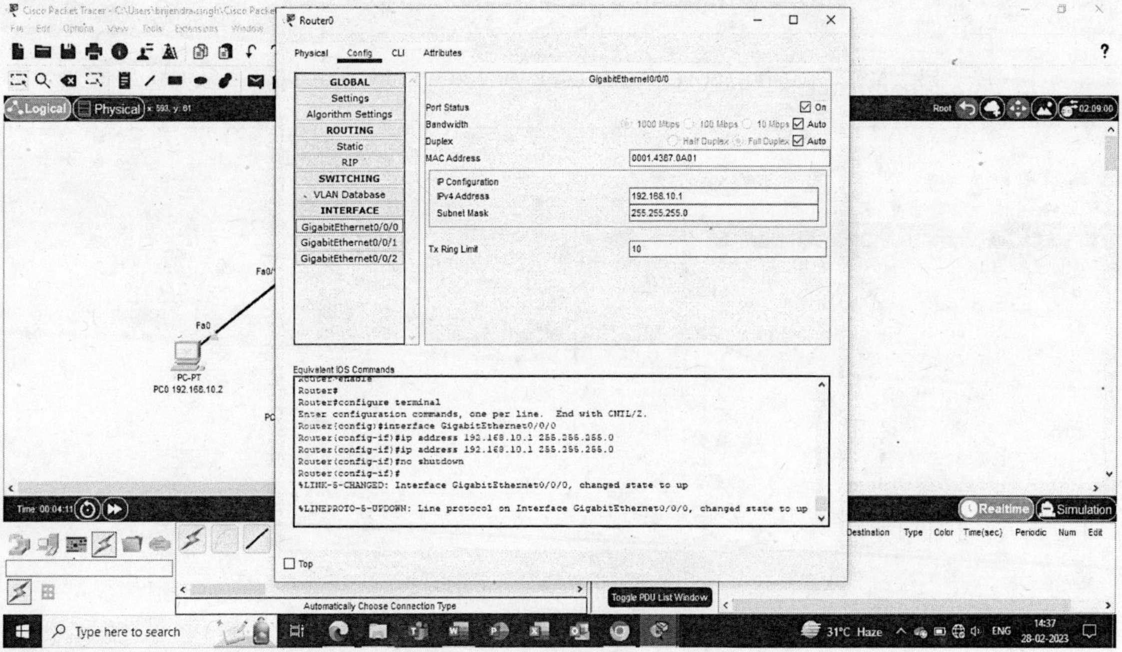

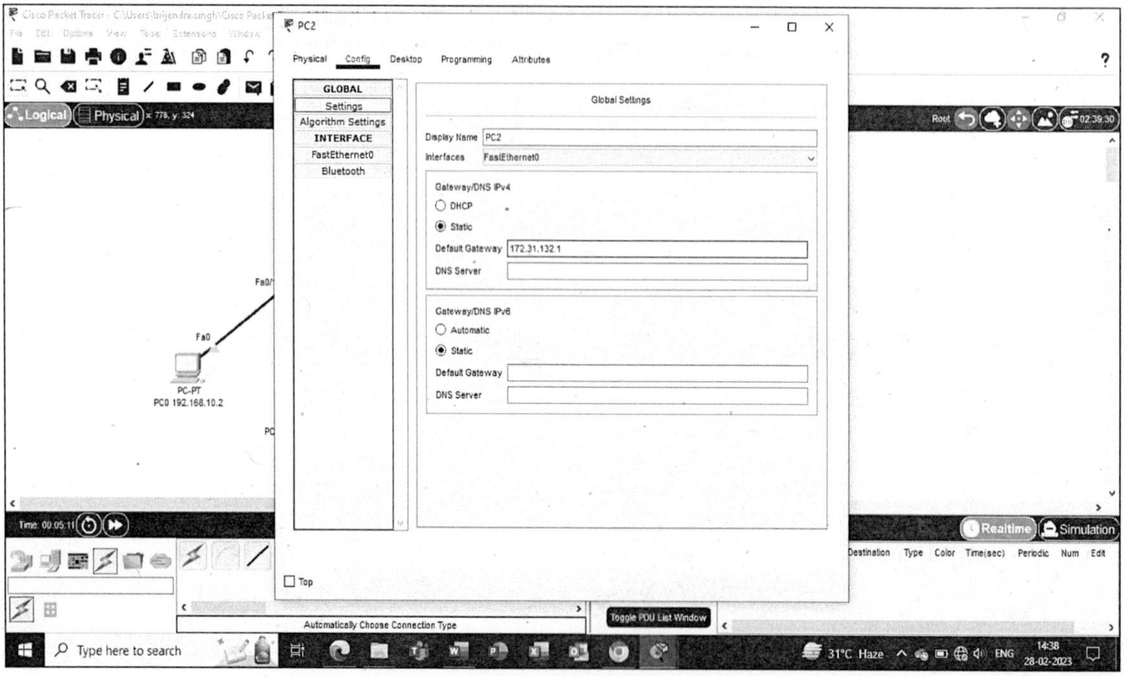

Fig. 5.8: Snapshot for setting router interface and PC default gateway

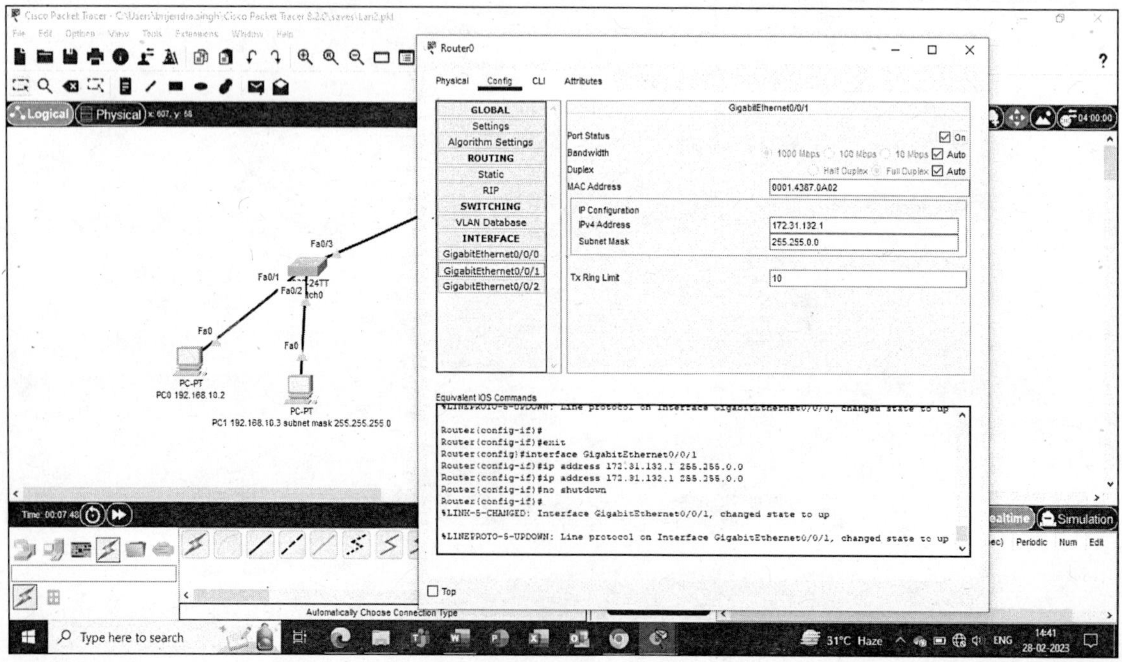

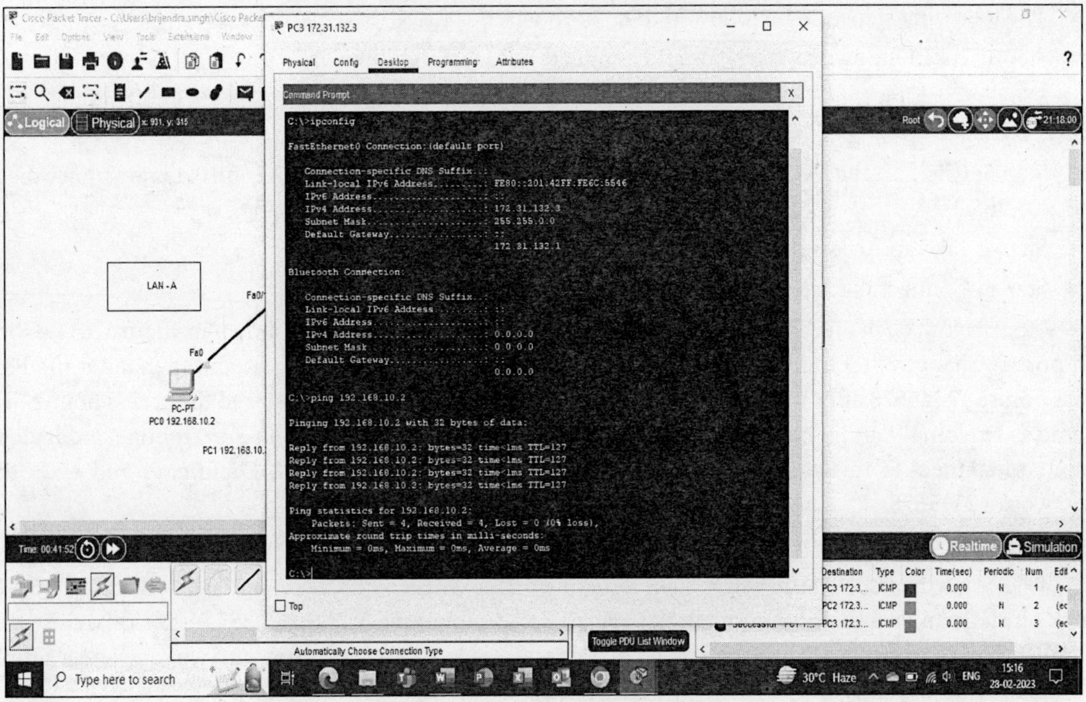

Fig. 5.9: Snapshot for setting router second interface and running ping and ipconfig command on command prompt

Aim -3

Setting up a small wireless LAN in the Lab

Here for the Wireless setting, we are using the static IPv4 address and subnet mask setting (it can be dynamic by using DHCP). We are creating a simple wireless network that has 2 PCs connected to a switch. An access point is connected to the switch. One smartphone and two laptops are connected to the access point.

The physical connection looks, as in **Figure 5.10**.

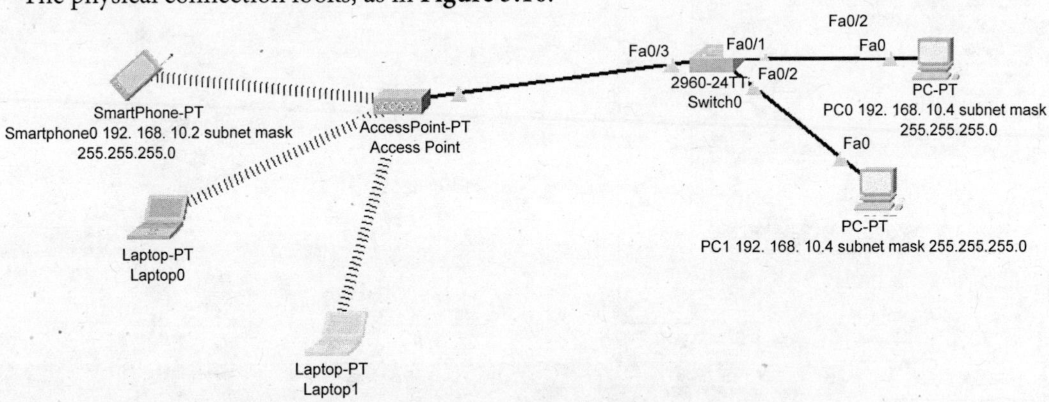

Fig. 5.10: Wireless LAN with three wireless devices

The following steps can be followed to create a wireless LAN.

Step 1: Take One switch, two PCs and connect them through the wire.

Step 2: Click on the PC0. Select the static and set the IPv4 address 192.168.10.3 and subnet mask 255.255.255.0

Step 3: Click on the PC1. Select the static and set the IPv4 address 192.168.10.4 and subnet mask 255.255.255.0

Step 4: Take an Access point, one smartphone, and two laptops

Step 5: Connect the access point to the switch through a wire

Step 6: Now, click on the Access point; a setting window will appear, as shown in **Figure 5.11.** Click on port 1. Change SSID to Diploma-4, Click on the authentication WPA2-PSK and then enter the PSK pass phrase 12345678 after that close this window. So, till now, we have configured the access point SSID name as Diploma-4 and password 12345678. Whenever a wireless device (our smartphone and laptop) wants to connect to this access point, they need to choose the SSID name Diploma-4 and enter the password 12345678.

Step 7: Now click on the smartphone, a setting window will appear, as shown in **Figure 5.12**

Click on wireless0, Set the SSID as Diploma-4, click on WPA2-PSK and put the password 12345678, click on static and set the IPv4 address 192.168.10.2 and subnet mask 255.255.255.0 after this, close this window. Now we can see that the smartphone is connected to the access point, and we can send a simple PDU packet to the PCs.

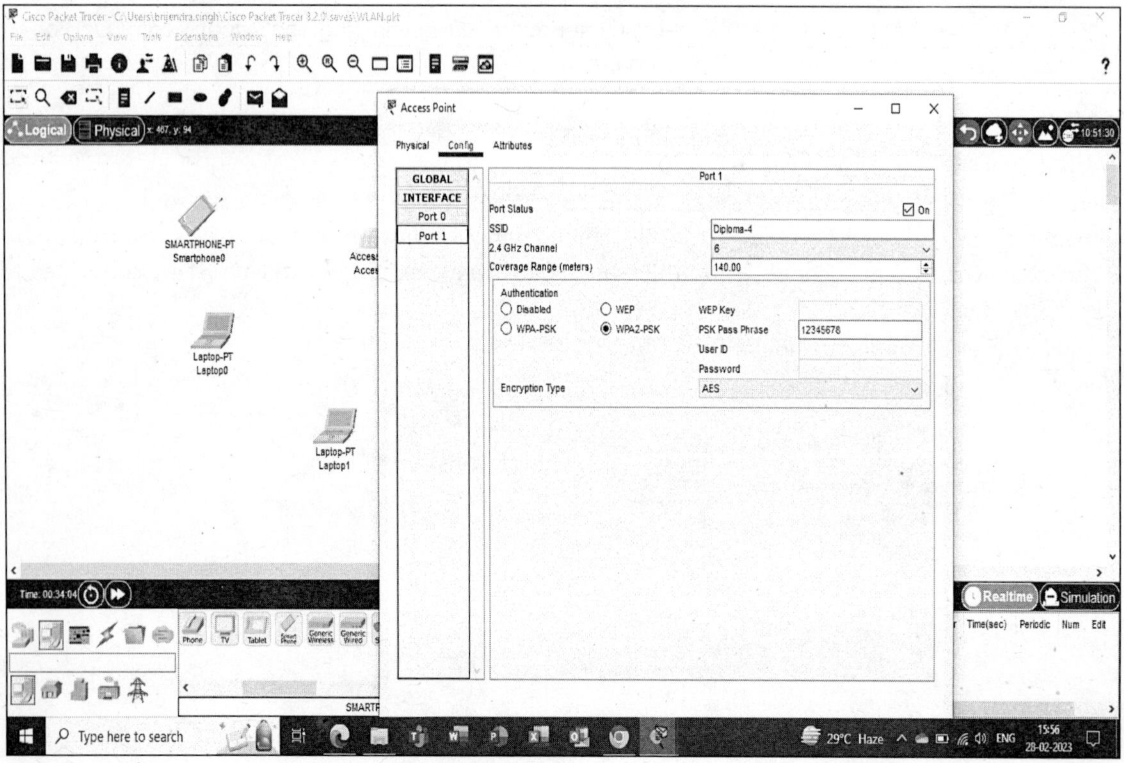

Fig. 5.11: Setting window of an access point

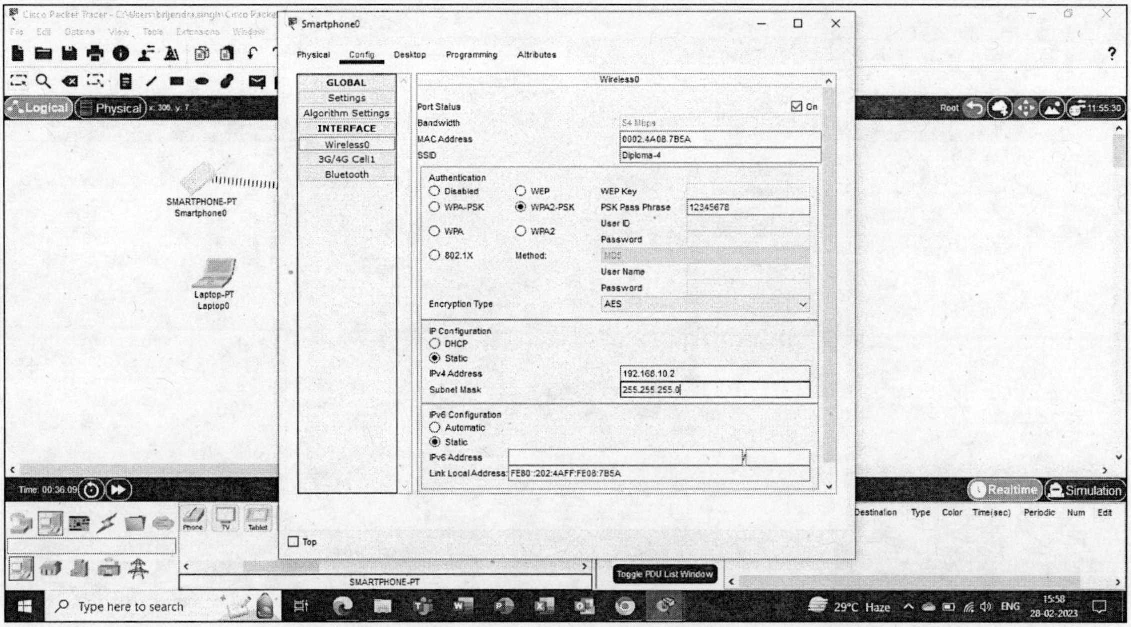

Fig. 5.12: Setting window of a smartphone

Step 8: To connect the laptop0, click on the laptop, a setting window will appear. By default, the wireless port is not in the laptop. We need to add a wireless port to the laptop. To do so, click on the physical, it will show the image of the laptop. There is a power button; click on the power button to switch off the laptop. Now remove the Ethernet port from the laptop. To remove the ethernet port, click on the ethernet port and drag it to the empty space on the screen; it will be removed. After that, click on the WPC300N, and drag WPC300N to the same place on the laptop image where the ethernet port was. The wireless port will be added. **Figure 5.13** shows the options. Now click on the power button to switch on the laptop. **Figure 5.14** shows the setting of SSID, WAP2PSK, IP and subnet mask. After this, click on config tab and the wireless0. Now, set the SSID as Diploma-4, click on WPA2-PSK and enter the key 12345678, and click on static and put the IPv4 address 192.168.10.5 and subnet mask 255.255.255.0.

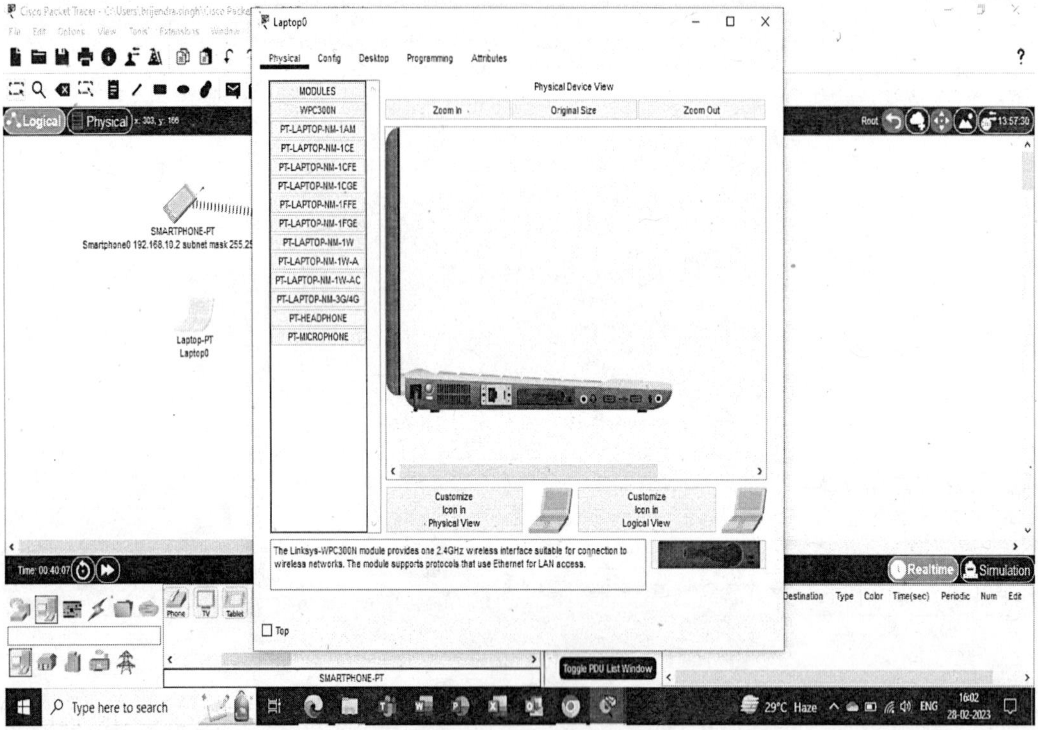

Fig. 5.13: Wireless port addition at the laptop

Step 9: Repeat the step 8 for laptop1 and set the SSID, Password key, IPv4 address 192.168.10.6 and subnet mask 255.255.255.0 as looking in **Figure 5.15.**

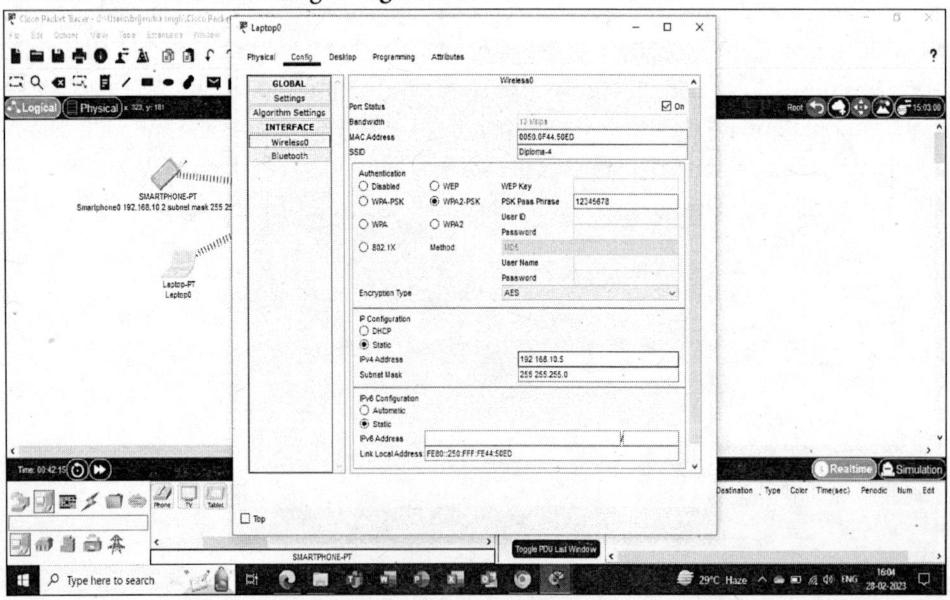

Fig. 5.14: Setting SSID, WPA2-PSK, IP address, and subnet mask in laptop

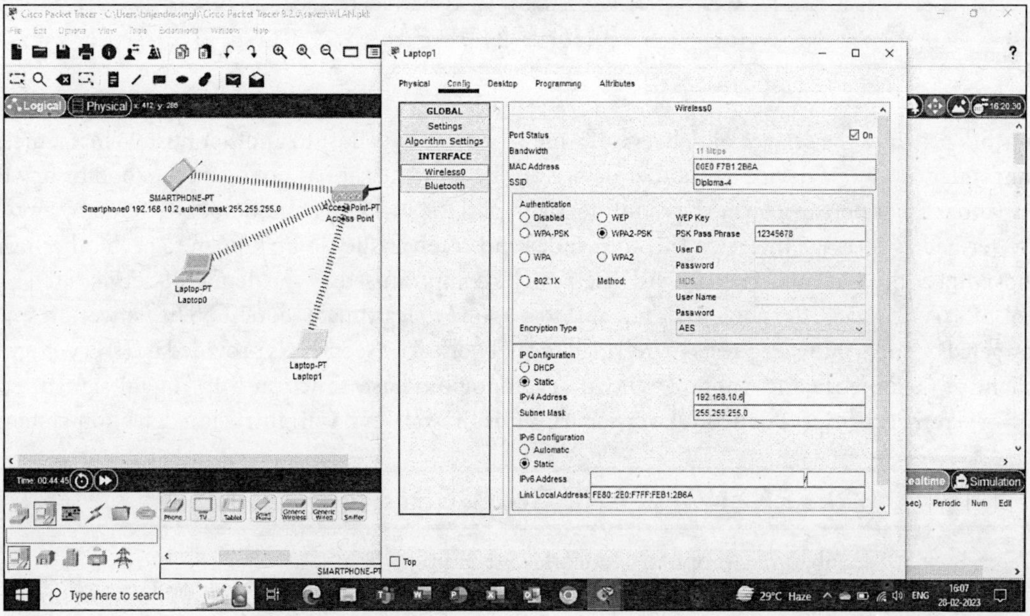

Fig. 5.15: Setting SSID, WPA2-PSK, IP address, and subnet mask in the second laptop

Now, all the devices are connected, and all the setting has been done. Now you can send a simple PDU message from any end device to any end device in the network. It will show the successful status if the message is delivered successfully, as shown in **Figure 5.16** at right bottom corner.

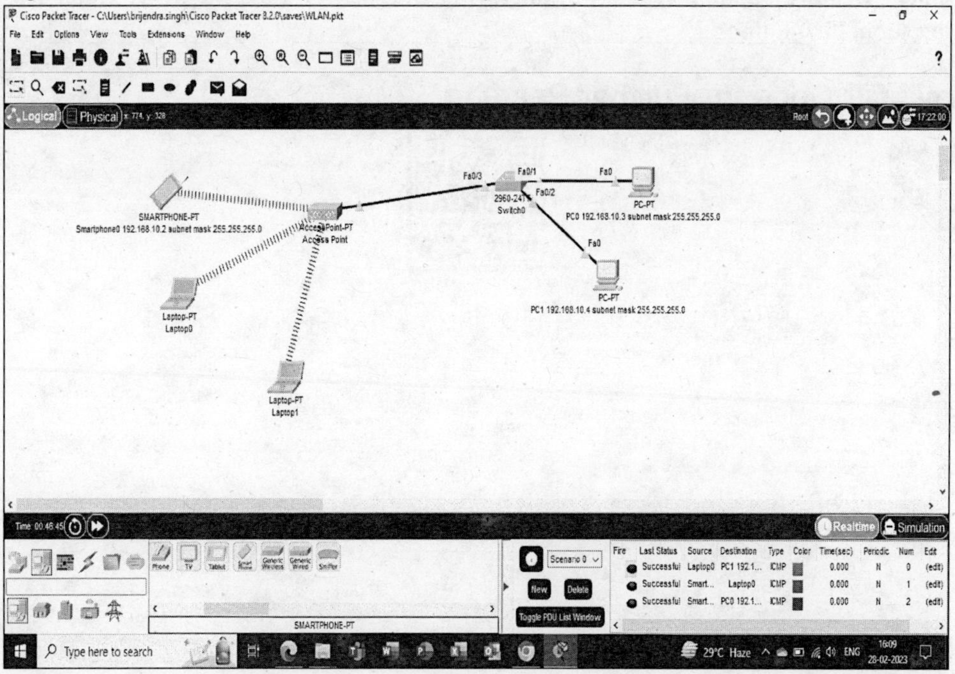

Fig. 5.16: A snapshot of sending simple PDU from smartphone and laptop to PC

KNOW MORE

Security

A network provides the service of delivery of a message from one host to another host. When a message is transmitted from one device to another device, (i) the message should not be understood by any third entity (program or person), termed as confidentiality, (ii) the message should not be altered by any third entity, termed as message integrity, (iii) the sender and receiver should be known to each other termed as end-point authentication. The network itself can be compromised by the denial-of-service attack. In a denial-of-service attack, the network is not able to respond to legitimate requests. The network resources are targeted by superfluous requests to overload the network. The security is provided by (i) cryptography mechanism (symmetric and public key), (ii) cryptographic hash function, (iii) digital signature, (iv) transport layer security, (v) network layer security, (vi) firewall, and (vii) intrusion detection system.

REFERENCES AND SUGGESTED READINGS

1. Andrew S. Tanenbaum, Computer Networks, 5th Edition, Pearson
2. W. Richard Stevens, TCP/IP Illustrated, Volume-1, Addision Wesley, Second Edition
3. James F. Kurose and Keith W. Ross, Computer Networking: A Top–Down Approach, Pearson, Eight Edition
4. Behrouz A. Forouzan and Firouz Mosharraf, Computer Networks: A Top-Down Approach, Mc Graw Hill Education, Special Indian Edition 2012
5. William Stalling, Computer Networking with Internet Protocols and Technology, Pearson Education, First Edition

Dynamic QR Code for Further Reading

REFERENCES FOR FURTHER LEARNING

1. Cloud Native Data Center Networking by Dinesh G. Dutt Released November 2019, Publisher(s): O'Reilly Media, Inc. ISBN: 9781492045601
2. Foundations of Modern Networking by William Stallings Pearson Education India; 1st edition (7 June 2016), ISBN-13: ⊠ 978-9332573864
3. Cryptography and Network Security - Principles and Practice by Stallings William, Pearson Education; Seventh edition (30 June 2017) , Seventh Edition, ISBN-13: ⊠ 978-9332585225
4. Making Sense of Cybersecurity, by Thomas Kranz, Manning Publications Co, ISBN 9781617298004
5. Ns-3 network simulator https://www.nsnam.org/

CO AND PO ATTAINMENT TABLE

Course outcomes (COs) for this course can be mapped with the programme outcomes (POs) after the completion of the course and a correlation can be made for the attainment of POs to analyze the gap. After proper analysis of the gap in the attainment of POs necessary measures can be taken to overcome the gaps.

Table for CO and PO attainment

Course Outcomes	Attainment of Programme Outcomes (1- Weak Correlation; 2- Medium correlation; 3- Strong Correlation)											
	PO-1	PO-2	PO-3	PO-4	PO-5	PO-6	PO-7	PO-8	PO-9	PO-10	PO-11	PO-12
CO-1												
CO-2												
CO-3												
CO-4												
CO-5												
CO-6												

The data filled in the above table can be used for gap analysis.

INDEX